by Lillian S. Freehof

Illustrated by Seymour R. Kaplan

PHILADELPHIA

The Jewish Publication Society of America

STORIES OF
King Solomon

COPYRIGHT ©, 1955, BY

THE JEWISH PUBLICATION SOCIETY OF AMERICA

LIBRARY OF CONGRESS CATALOG CARD NUMBER: 55-8423

Library of Congress Cataloging-in-Publication Data

Freehof, Lillian S. (Lillian Simon).,1906 –
Stories of King Solomon / by Lillian S. Freehof;
illustrated by Seymour R. Kaplan.
p. cm.
Previously published: Philadelphia: Jewish Publication Society
of America, c 1955.
ISBN 0 – 8276 – 0566 – 8
1. Solomon, King of Israel – Juvenile literature. 2. Jews – Kings and rulers –
Biography – Juvenile literature. 3. Bible. O.T. – Biography – Juvenile
literature. 4. Bible stories, English – O.T. I. Kaplan, Seymour R.,
ill. II. Title

BS580. S6F7 1995	95 – 22098
296. 1'42 – DC20	CIP

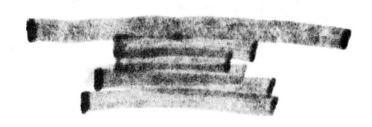

DEDICATED
IN DEEP DEVOTION
TO THE MEMORY OF OUR DEAR

GOLDA

Preface

Stories of King Solomon, although coming from the same sources, differ from *Stories of King David* in mood and spirit. The David stories are nearly all of courage; the Solomon stories of cleverness and magic. The David stories are stories of fighting; those of Solomon of building. The David stories centered around Judea and the land of the Philistines; the Solomon stories tell of far travels on wings of eagles and magic carpets.

These magic travels to many lands explain why the Solomon stories planted themselves so deeply in the folklore of different peoples, so much so that St. John D. Seymour, in *Tales of King Solomon* (London, Humphrey Milford, 1924, page 7) said in his preface: "Some of them (stories of King Solomon) have been drawn from places so far apart as Ireland and the Malay peninsula."

The midrashic-talmudic stories, derived chiefly from Louis Ginzberg's *Legends of the Jews,* in themselves cover a vast area and give us a world-wide mood of the Solomon legends wherever they are found.

The author hopes that these stories which reflect the ideal of wisdom so deeply a part of Jewish folk-lore, against the background of opulent splendor not too frequently a part of Jewish experience, will bring joy to many readers.

The vast folklore treasury of the Midrash would be closed to the average reader but for the selfless devotion of the late Dr. Louis Ginzberg in collating the myths and legends from all Jewish sources into his monumental work, *Legends of the Jews.* The student of folklore must always acknowledge a debt to him.

To the artist, Mr. Seymour R. Kaplan, goes my gratitude for his interesting and beautiful interpretation of the stories through his pictures.

And to my dear husband, Dr. Solomon B. Freehof, who first introduced me to the charm and the fascination of the Midrash, and who has never wavered in his interest in my continued studies, I am especially grateful.

L.S.F.

Eve of Rosh Hashanah, 5716.
October 16, 1955.

Contents

Forty-Nine Gates

LONG, LONG AGO, DAVID, THE SON OF JESSE, ruled as King of Israel. When he became very old, he knew that the time had come to choose one of his sons to be king after him. But he had several sons and how was he to choose amongst them? He then decided that the future king must pass two tests. He had to be able to wear the King's Crown. But, even more important, he had to answer all the questions which all the scholars were to put to him. By these answers David would know which son had the greatest wisdom and, if the Crown would fit him, that son would be worthy of becoming the new king.

All of David's sons, of course, wanted to be king. Absalom and Adonijah, Chileab and Amnon heard about the two tests, but they paid little attention to them. Certainly, they thought, anybody could wear the King's Crown. As for the test of wisdom, each one had a different attitude towards it.

8

Chileab, it is true, was studious, but he was positive that he could never be king, though he longed for it. He knew that he was too shy to face the wise men and give the right answers. Amnon was too busy having a good time to be bothered with the whole matter. Adonijah, certain that he would be king, hired men to run before him everywhere he went, proclaiming, "Make way for King Adonijah." But Absalom, not too sure of passing the tests, and wanting to make certain he would be king, began laying plans to incite a rebellion and overthrow King David.

Solomon, the King's youngest son, had listened carefully to King David's announcement. Although he was only twelve years old, he was not too shy but not too sure. He was not too reckless but not too confident. He hoped and prayed that he could grow wise enough to answer all the questions which the scholars might put to him.

Now Solomon had always been a friend of the animals. His best friend was a big, white Eagle who used to come into the royal garden every morning, carry Solomon on one of his huge wings, fly him about, and show him many parts of the world never seen by any human.

The morning after his father made the announcement, Solomon decided that perhaps his friend the white Eagle could show him where to find wisdom. He went out into the garden and there, already waiting for him, was his feathered friend. Solomon patted the bald white head and said, half-jokingly,

"Today you must take me to the place where I can learn wisdom."

He laughed, knowing the Eagle could not understand his language. He mounted the wing of the Eagle and the huge bird soared gracefully upward into the sky, flying on and on until he came to the place where the ravens had

their nests. Looking down into the nests, young Solomon was surprised to see little white baby ravens and big black-feathered ravens. Then he nodded, understanding at once that baby ravens are always white-feathered and that as they grow older they shed their white feathers and grow black ones instead.

This was interesting, of course, but Solomon was sure that this was not wisdom. It was only knowledge. He wasn't quite sure yet what wisdom was. Knowledge, he knew, was the learning of certain facts. But what was wisdom?

The Eagle carried him home. He woke early the following morning and went into the garden, and there again, his friend the Eagle waited for him. Again, Solomon said, jokingly,

"Take me where I can learn wisdom, O my wise friend."

He mounted on the wing of the Eagle and they flew aloft for a long, long time until they came to the desert. There the Eagle circled round and round until his keen eyes saw what he was looking for. He swooped down to a spot in the desert where a large bird stood all alone. The bird seemed to be burning up! It *was* burning up. A gentle fire, not a raging flame — just a slow, gentle blaze — was covering the bird's body from the tip of the head to the very smallest toes, and, as the animal burned, it dissolved into white ashes. Then, before Solomon's very eyes, from the midst of the ashes there emerged a small white bird. Suddenly Solomon realized what he had witnessed.

Once he had heard his father tell him and his brothers about the wonderful bird, the Phoenix, which lived for one thousand years. When it reached that old, old age, it was consumed gently and slowly by a fire which burned it into white ashes, and from the white ashes came the new baby Phoenix which then grew larger and larger and lived for one thousand years.

Solomon was overjoyed to have seen the new Phoenix emerge from the ashes. He knew that what he had seen today he would never see again because, of course, he could never live to be a thousand and twelve years old! But his excitement was mixed with sadness because, while he knew he had witnessed something wonderful, he knew that he had gained only knowledge. Now he knew that what he had heard about the Phoenix was true. But did this add to his wisdom?

The Eagle flew him home again. That night he fell asleep earlier than usual, worn out from the excitement and the wonder of the day's journey.

While he slept he dreamed, and in his dream God spoke with him, and said, "Solomon, O Solomon, you may have one wish. Wish for the thing you

want most in the world. Do you want long life? Do you yearn for great wealth? Do you desire honor? What one wish may I bestow upon you?"

And Solomon answered, "O Lord, all those things I would like to have; but more than anything, I yearn for wisdom. O Lord, grant me wisdom."

In Solomon's dream, the Voice faded, and on the echo of the wind came a whisper,

"You may have your wish, O Solomon. But first you must find the forty-nine gates of wisdom. When you will find them and enter them all, you will become wise, very wise."

Solomon awoke the next morning and immediately remembered his dream. He could have one wish and he had wished for wisdom. The Lord would grant him his wish if he could find the forty-nine gates. Where were they? Where to look for them? How would he find them? Who could help him?

After he had eaten his breakfast, he went out into the garden and saw two birds on the ground, chirping merrily. He stood and listened to the birds, and he thought, these funny little sounds the birds are making, certainly they must be bird-language. Surely the birds would not just make the sounds unless they meant something. *They* seem to understand each other. Perhaps if I tried to know what is of interest to the birds, what they think about, how they live, perhaps I would understand their language too.

So for the next few hours he searched for birds everywhere, in the garden, at the brook, near the river. And he watched them, and studied them. He saw that their main concerns were what everybody's were: where to build their home, how to find food, how to take care of their children. And then Solomon said to himself, *that* is wisdom! Watching the young ravens shed their white feathers and grow black ones, that was knowledge which I know and can teach to someone else. But to understand someone else's life, even if it is only a bird's, that is wisdom! Thus, without leaving his father's garden, he travelled through one gate of wisdom when he learned the life and the language of the birds.

The next day, Solomon said to himself, now I must find another gate of wisdom. He happened to go through the Music Room where his father was playing his lute while composing a psalm. Solomon had always heard the sounds which the strings made, but they had never meant anything to him before. Now he listened carefully, trying to understand what the music itself tried to say to him, or what his father was trying to express through the music. Was this sad music? Was it happy music? Did it teach him anything?

12

And then Solomon, after puzzling for hours, realized that to learn to play a song, to know what chords to play, which fingers to strike, what rhythm to count, that was gathering knowledge. But the wisdom to be learned from the music was different. It was to try to understand what the artist wished to say, what dreams and hopes he expressed through his music. Thus gradually Solomon travelled through the Gate of Art, and acquired the wisdom of understanding the artist.

The next day, going towards the stables, Solomon saw a young horse writhing and thrashing in pain. He ran forward to try to help the doctor hold the horse, and he saw what medicines the doctor was using to try to ease the pain of the animal. But while he helped and while he watched, Solomon looked at the animal and saw the fear reflected in its eyes and felt its heart beating fast with the pain, and Solomon knew pity. He knew that what the doctor was doing to help the animal was based on his knowledge of what was wrong with the horse and what medicines to use. But suddenly Solomon knew, too, that having that knowledge wasn't enough. It was just as important to understand another living being's pain and to try to help it get over that pain. That was wisdom.

So with one step, Solomon walked through the Gate of Mercy and learned the wisdom of pity and the wisdom of healing.

And thus it went, day after day. Fulfilling the promise of his dream, Solomon travelled through every gate of wisdom, all forty-nine of them, until he became, in all truth, the wisest person who had ever lived.

But no one knew that yet. The wisdom that he learned he kept in his heart. And to himself he kept repeating,

"How much better it is to get wisdom than gold."

Then came the day when King David assembled his court, and the law court of seventy wise men, the Sanhedrin, and every scholar in the kingdom. The time had come to test his sons to see which one was worthy to rule after him. All the sons were there, of course, each one seated on a small golden throne. Amnon looked silly because he was still dreaming about yesterday's party and thinking of the one he would go to that evening. Chileab looked frightened because he knew he would not have the courage to answer the questions. Adonijah looked scornful because he didn't really believe his father would decide on the future king in this manner. And Absalom looked rebellious because he felt that, as the oldest son, the kingship should come to him without tests and without question.

But Solomon sat quietly, waiting.

And the questioning began.

Every scholar and every councillor and every nobleman was permitted to ask each son one question and, if the prince questioned failed to give the correct answer, he was out of the competition. Amnon, of course, failed on the very first question. Chileab failed on the second because he was too frightened to think clearly. Adonijah went as far as the fifth question. But Absalom answered eight questions correctly before he failed on the ninth.

Then they began to question Solomon. And Solomon answered every question correctly. The seventy wise men of the supreme court each asked a question. Every Levite priest, every nobleman, every scholar, every man connected with the court asked a question. And Solomon answered every one. Every person in the throne room sat up straighter and straighter in amazement. Only King David took it calmly. He was not surprised. Only King David smiled. Then, finally, he said,

"Young Solomon has answered all the questions. He has fulfilled the first requirement."

Absalom jumped to his feet, intending to protest, but his father commanded him to be seated. Adonijah jumped to his feet, but sat down again when a stronger voice than his interrupted. It was the President of the Sanhedrin who now protested.

"Solomon is only twelve years old, Your Majesty. How can you, O David, name him as the king to rule after you?"

King David smiled and said, "Has he failed to answer any questions?"

"No, Your Majesty," the President answered. "But the questions put to him only tested his knowledge. He has not given evidence of true, deep wisdom."

"Then you have my permission," said the King, "to question him further."

Thereupon, the President of the Sanhedrin turned to Solomon and said,

"Your Highness, with the King's permission, I must now test your wisdom. Please answer this question: Who is a dangerous person?"

And Solomon said, "A fool is, sir, because he causes much mischief. It is well known, Your Honor, that the father of a fool has no joy."

"Good, very good," King David said, smiling. "And tell us this, my son: What does the Lord hate most?"

"The Lord hates a liar," Solomon said. "And He hates a boastful man, and He hates a wicked person who is always planning evil."

14

Then the President said to Solomon, "Who among men is most mighty?"

And Solomon answered, "He that is slow to anger, for a soft answer turneth away wrath."

"Now surely," King David said. "Now surely Solomon has shown wisdom as well as knowledge. He has answered every question which was put to him. The lad is full of wisdom. He has proven that he is wise enough to rule as king after me. Now there is one more test to which he must be put. He must take this crown off my head."

"But that is easy to do, father," shouted Absalom. "Anyone can lift the crown from your head."

"Anyone?" David asked, smiling. "No, not anyone, my son Absaolm. This crown has the Divine Name written on it. Only he who is to be the rightful ruler of Israel will have the strength to lift this crown. But, my son Absalom, since you think that anyone can lift it, I shall give each one of my sons the opportunity to try. Come, Absalom, you may try first."

Absalom strode forward confidently and tried to lift off the King's crown, but, to his amazement, the crown stayed firmly in place. Adonijah tried, even more roughly than Absalom. And Chileab tried, but more timidly. And none of them could remove David's crown. Amnon, bored, didn't even make the attempt.

Then Solomon walked forward, bowed to his father, smiled, and with the tips of his fingers he lifted David's crown off his head and placed it on his own.

The noblemen and the scholars, the priests and the seventy members of the court, broke into a loud cheer for Solomon, and one nobleman cried out,

"Live long, King David. And may God bless Solomon, your successor!"

The Unhatched Egg

One day in the crisp autumn, in King David's apple orchard, two of his servants were busy pruning the trees. The morning passed quickly and soon it was time for the noon-day meal. The two men sat down in the shade of a tree and Ezra, the older one, began to unpack his lunch. Amos, his friend, rested his chin on his hand, and sighed.

"What's the trouble?" Ezra asked. "Toothache?"

"Oh no," Amos answered. "There's no trouble with my teeth except that there's nothing for them to bite into. I have no food."

"Too bad," Ezra said, munching on a crust of bread.

Amos, looking slyly at the food in Ezra's package, said, "Would you give me an egg, Ezra?"

"Humph!" snorted Ezra. "I might, if you pay me."

"But I have no money," Amos pleaded. "I'm very hungry, friend Ezra."

"Well, I'll give you one egg," Ezra said, "if you promise to give me whatever the egg produces, whether it is one chicken or ten chickens."

"I promise," Amos said, eagerly snatching the egg out of Ezra's hand, cracking it open and eating it before Ezra could say "eggshell."

16

A few months went by and Amos had not repaid the loan. Ezra looked for him one day and found him in the sheepcote, tending the sheep.

"Ho, there, Amos," Ezra said. "I've come to collect what you owe me."

"And I have it right here for you," Amos said, taking a hard-boiled egg out of his knapsack and handing it to Ezra. "Here is an egg in return for the egg you gave me."

"Do you call that repaying the debt?" Ezra shouted. "You promised to give me everything the egg produced. You've got to pay your debt."

"I have," Amos said. "I owed you one egg and I've returned it."

"Thief," Ezra shouted. "Thief, pay me what you owe me!"

"I don't owe you anything more!" Amos shouted back.

The Chief Shepherd came hurrying out of the sheepcote. "Here, here," he said. "What's the trouble? Your shouting is frightening the sheep."

"He won't pay his debt to me!" Ezra shouted.

"I have repaid it!" Amos shouted in turn.

"Quiet! Quiet!" the Chief Shepherd yelled. "You can't settle your quarrel here. King David is holding court right now. Take your case to him and leave my sheep in peace."

The two men hurried away from the sheepcote, went to the palace and, after telling the guard they had a case to bring before the King, they went in and told the Court Recorder and he listed their case for the King to hear that morning.

King David was sitting on his throne, listening carefully to each problem which came before his court, while his son Solomon sat next to him and listened just as carefully.

Finally the Court Recorder called the case of Ezra and Amos. The two men stepped up before King David and bowed. Then Ezra said,

"Your Majesty, I loaned Amos an egg after he promised to give me in return everything which the egg produced. And now he refuses to pay his debt. All he will give me is one egg, but that was not our bargain."

"Why do you not pay your debt?" King David asked Amos.

"I have repaid my debt, Your Majesty," Amos answered. "I gave Ezra one egg in return for the egg he gave me. No chickens came out of the egg he gave me, because I ate the egg."

King David pondered for a moment, and then said, "If you promised to give him the chickens that egg would hatch, then you had no right to eat it.

17

Therefore you owe Ezra a great deal of money. From that egg could have come one chick, the chick could have laid eighteen eggs, each egg could have produced eighteen chicks, each chick could have laid eighteen eggs, and so on and so on. It's a complicated mathematical problem. The Court Treasurer will have to figure out how many chickens could have come out of the eggs which the chickens could have laid which came out of that one egg. You will have to pay an enormous amount of money to Ezra. Case dismissed."

Ezra smiled, turned and left the courtroom. Amos stood looking at King David in a dazed way.

"But . . ." he started to say.

He was not allowed to finish. "Clear the court, please," the Court Recorder ordered him. "Next case!"

Amos turned away and stumbled out of the court room, knowing that Ezra had tricked him and that King David had not understood the problem because it had not been properly presented to him. At the door he felt someone tug at his sleeve. It was Solomon, the King's son. He motioned Amos to follow him outside to the rose garden and there young Solomon turned to Amos and said,

"I know that your friend Ezra tricked you, Amos."

"He did, he did!" Amos insisted.

Solomon nodded. "And my father failed to ask you one question which would have settled the case in your favor."

Amos nodded.

"Now," Solomon said. "You cannot just go to King David and say, 'O King, you made a mistake.' You'll have to *show* him that he made a mistake. Now I have a plan in mind . . ."

He began to whisper, and Amos leaned over to hear the whole plan. When Solomon finished whispering, Amos straightened, smiled, and said,

"A good plan, young Solomon. Thank you very much. I shall follow your advice."

Just then the Court Treasurer came hurrying over to Amos. He was carrying a long sheet of parchment.

"I have figured out your debt to Ezra," he said. "You owe him one thousand gold pieces."

"One thousand gold pieces!" Amos exclaimed. "I have no gold pieces at all. How will I ever pay him!"

18

"That's not my concern." The Court Treasurer shrugged and hurried away.

"How will I pay him one thousand gold pieces?" Amos asked again.

"You won't have to pay him even one gold piece if you follow my advice," Solomon said.

"Yes, yes," Amos said eagerly. "I shall do just as you say. Just promise me that you will bring King David past my little garden patch tomorrow morning."

"I promise," young Solomon said.

Amos hurried away to his little cottage. He put water in a big pot and put the pot on the fire. When the water in the pot began to boil, into the pot he threw two measures of peas and let them stay there until they were well cooked. Then he went to bed.

As soon as the sun rose the next morning, Amos got out of bed, dressed and ate his breakfast. Then he took the big pot of peas which he had cooked the night before and went outdoors to the small garden patch near his cottage. He cleared one square of ground, dug it up and prepared it for sowing. Then he waited.

He waited until he heard the sound of bugles which meant that the King was approaching. He waited until the King's pages came near where he was working, and then he began to sow the cooked peas into the ground. As King David and young Solomon approached Amos, the King, looking to see what he was doing, saw in an instant that the peas Amos was sowing were cooked peas.

King David stopped.

"Here, Amos," he said. "What are you doing? Why do you sow cooked peas? You know they will not produce any fruit."

"They will produce as much fruit, Your Majesty," Amos said respectfully, "as the egg which Ezra gave me would produce chickens."

"The egg which Ezra gave you?" the King asked, puzzled. "What are you talking about, Amos?"

"Your Majesty," Amos said. "Yesterday you decided the case against me, saying that out of the egg which Ezra gave me could have come one chicken which could have laid eighteen eggs out of which could have come eighteen chickens . . ."

"Yes, yes," interrupted King David. "I remember. Don't repeat."

"And I say to you, O King," Amos said, "that no chickens could have come out of the egg which Ezra gave me any more than a single pea will grow out of these peas which I am now planting."

"Go on," King David said slowly, beginning to realize what Amos would say. "Why couldn't the egg which Ezra gave you have produced any chickens?"

"Because, Your Majesty," Amos said. "That egg was a hard-boiled egg."

King David glared at Amos, then he turned to stare at young Solomon. "Was the planting of these cooked peas your idea?"

"Yes, father," Solomon said.

Then, suddenly, King David smiled. He turned back to Amos and laughed.

"I should have asked you if the egg was cooked or not," he said, laughing again. "You win. The case against you is dismissed. You do not owe Ezra anything except one hard-boiled egg."

The King and young Solomon turned and went back to the palace and Amos went back to his work in the sheepcote, smiling to himself and murmuring,

"What a wonderful king that young Solomon will be some day."

The Flying Sack

Caleb, the Carpenter, was a poor man but he was blessed with three lovely little daughters. But, since his wife was dead, there was no one to take care of them. The oldest of the girls, Deborah, had to take care of the house and her two little sisters. They were all as pretty as princesses and Caleb would have liked to give them a palace to live in and beautiful clothes to wear. But, alas, he was so poor that sometimes they didn't even have enough food to eat.

One morning, bright and early, Caleb left Deborah in charge of the house and her sisters, while he went to the market to buy a sack of flour. He never liked to leave the children alone for long, so, after he bought the flour, he decided to go home by the shorter route which was past the open sea.

As he left the market, the sun was shining brightly and a light breeze was blowing. He walked very fast, the sack of flour hoisted on his shoulder. He looked out to the sea and along the ocean front, watching the waves pile high one on the other and the whitecaps dance in the sun. It was still and calm where he was walking along the shore, and he enjoyed looking out at the rough sea while he walked on the white sand in the mild air.

Then, suddenly, before he realized what was happening, all around him a sharp wind began to blow. Caleb bent his head against it, half closing his eyes to keep the sand out, holding on tightly to the sack of flour on his shoulder. But the wind blew stronger and stronger until it was almost a gale, and Caleb bent double to keep from being knocked over by its force. But still he clutched the sack of flour on his shoulder. And then, suddenly, the wind blew a terrific gust which, like huge fingers grabbing, lifted the sack of flour right off Caleb's shoulder!

He cried out and tried to snatch at it, but away it sailed, on the crest of the strong wind, high out over the sea. Caleb, dumbfounded, stood and watched it, expecting it to sink down into the green waves and be lost from sight. But instead, it seemed to sail in the air without ever touching the water. The wind around Caleb seemed to float out to sea with the sack of flour, and then, once again, the air around him was soft and calm. Poor Caleb watched his sack of flour floating, floating out to sea. He watched it until it was just a tiny speck on the horizon, and then it faded away, completely out of sight.

Caleb was left standing on the shore, watching the green-white waves, and his shoulder was light and his hands were empty. He couldn't go back to the market and buy another sack of flour. He had no more money. What he would do to feed his three hungry little girls, he didn't know. With a heavy heart and shuffling footsteps, he returned to his poor, humble home and told his little girls what had happened to the sack of flour.

The two smaller girls began to cry because they were very hungry. But Deborah stood listening to her father and thinking. After he stopped talking, she was still thinking, very hard, her pretty face puckered with a frown, so hard was she thinking. And then her face cleared and she smiled and said,

"Why, father, I know what you should do. You should go to the old King David and tell him your story and he will give you the money for another sack of flour."

"Why should he do that?" Caleb asked. "He didn't throw my sack of flour into the sea. It was the wind that snatched it away."

"But King David rules this whole kingdom," said Deborah. "And so he rules over the wind that blew your sack of flour into the sea. You should go to him, Father, you should."

"Yes, yes, go to King David," the two little hungry sisters cried.

"Well, I guess I can't lose anything by going," Caleb said.

And so he went to the palace where King David was holding court. The

22

King was sitting on his throne, and next to him sat the young Solomon who would be King some day. He was listening to all the lawsuits which came before his father's court. Soon it was time for Caleb to present his case.

He bowed to the King, and then he bowed to young Solomon.

"Your Majesty," he said. "I am a very poor man with three little daughters to feed. Today I took the last of my money and went to the market and bought a sack of flour. In order to get home quickly, I walked along the shore of the sea. And along came a strong wind which lifted the sack of flour from my shoulder and carried it out to sea. Now, Your Majesty, I have neither the flour nor the money."

King David shook his head. "A sad story. But I do not see why you have come to me since it was the wind that robbed you. However, you have always been a loyal subject and I shall give you the money you spent, so you can buy more flour."

The King ordered the Royal Treasurer to give the man the amount of money he had spent on the sack of flour. The man thanked the king, took the money, went to the market, bought another sack of flour, went home through the woods this time, and his little girls were all very happy because now they would have bread and food to eat.

Back in the palace, young Solomon was talking with his father.

"I think it was kind of you, father, to give Caleb some money to buy more flour," he said. "But why do you not call the wind to account for his wicked deed?"

"Call the wind to account?" King David laughed. "And how would I do that? And what good would it do? Suppose I did summon the West Wind, if I could, and I said, 'Here now, see here, what do you mean by robbing that poor man? Pay him back in gold or I shall put you in jail?' Imagine putting the wind in jail!" King David laughed again.

"Now, don't laugh, father," young Solomon said. "Of course you can't put the wind in jail. And of course he can't pay the man back in money. But Caleb told us that the sack of flour floated off. It didn't sink into the sea. So it may be that the wind took the flour for some purpose of his own. Then you should make him return it."

Then King David showed annoyance. He said almost angrily, "Now, Solomon, don't be childish. Enough of this foolishness. You know I cannot conjure the wind to appear before me . . ."

Solomon interrupted, saying quietly, "I can."

King David looked at him, and said slowly, "You can?"

Solomon nodded. "I know the language of the birds and the beasts and the wind."

"Very well then," King David said. "Summon the West Wind."

Solomon rose and walked to the west window and opened it wide. Then he spoke softly in words that sounded like "Oooo, whoo," the sound a wind makes when it is blowing gently. Then he waited. And suddenly into the room blew a strong, sharp wind; and near Solomon wind-words whistled which he understood.

"I came at your bidding, O Solomon," the West Wind said.

"Thank you for coming," Solomon answered. "I have called you here to

ask you to give an account of yourself. Why did you steal Caleb's sack of flour?"

"I did not steal it, O Solomon. I borrowed it," the Wind answered.

"Borrowed it?" Solomon asked. "Do you intend to return it?"

"No," the Wind answered. "I guess I shouldn't have said 'borrowed'; but I don't know what else to say. I didn't steal it, really, but I did have use for that flour."

"Now what use does the West Wind have with a sack of flour?" young Solomon asked, half angrily.

"Listen, O Solomon, and I shall tell you. Far, far, way out at sea, as I was blowing along earlier today, I came upon a big ship which was in trouble.

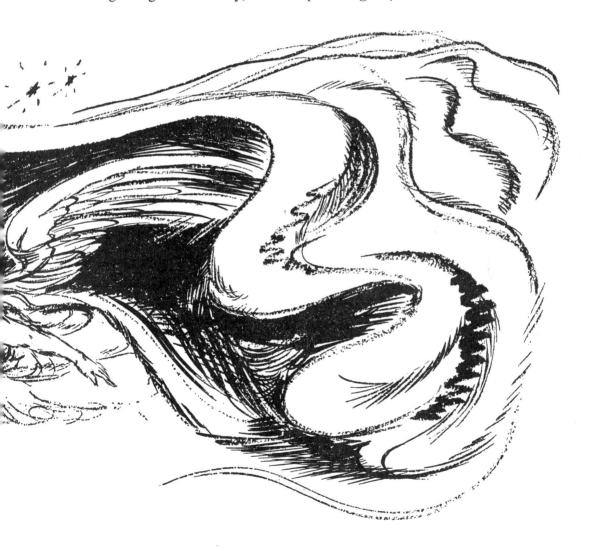

The ship had struck against a huge rock, and had sprung a leak. It was in danger of sinking, with its fifty-nine passengers and its cargo of spices and silver and precious cloth. So I blew off to the shore to find something to stop up that leak, and the first thing I saw was this man carrying a sack of flour."

"Yes, go on," Solomon said.

"I didn't have time to explain to the man what I needed the flour for," the West Wind said. "Besides, I was afraid he wouldn't understand my language. So I just grabbed the sack off his shoulder and blew back to that ship, and just in time! Five more minutes and she would have been beyond saving. But I stuffed that flour into the leak and it stopped it up, and the ship was saved!"

"Well done, O Wind!" exclaimed Solomon. "That was quick thinking on your part, and a noble deed. Well done."

"Good-bye," whistled the West Wind.

The wind-words stopped. The Wind blew away from the courtroom out through the west window, and the air in the room was calm and quiet once more. Solomon walked back to the throne and repeated to his father the conversation he had had with the West Wind.

"Oh good," King David said. "Oh, well done. Then I am glad I gave Caleb the money to buy another sack of flour. And I am glad the Wind saved that ship with her passengers and precious cargo."

Thereupon everyone — Caleb and his pretty daughters, King David and young Solomon — forgot the whole incident.

Several weeks passed.

One day when King David was sitting in the rose-garden composing a new psalm, and young Solomon lay stretched on the grass in front of him writing a few wise proverbs, the King's chief councillor came, walking slowly over the grass, hesitant about disturbing the King. He waited a moment until David had rested his hand against the lute, quieting the strings. The Councillor said timidly,

"Your Majesty, forgive me for disturbing you. An urgent matter . . ."

"Yes, speak up," King David said kindly.

"There is a strange man here to see you. He is the captain of a ship. I have told him to come tomorrow morning when the court is in session. But he insists that he must speak with you at once."

"Very well," King David said. "Bring the man here."

The councillor hurried away, and in a few moments returned with a sea captain. The man bowed to the King, and stood before him looking like a beggar. His clothes were ragged and he looked very tired, as if he had not slept for a long time.

"I beg you to forgive my appearance, Your Majesty," he said. "But I have just brought my ship safely to harbor after many dangers and many hardships. I could not take the time to dress myself in fine garments because the matter I bring before you is of urgent concern."

"Very well," King David said. "Speak."

Young Solomon sat up and looked at the man carefully and then he began to smile, almost as if he knew what the man was going to say.

The captain spoke.

"Several weeks ago, while I was bringing my ship, laden with rich cargo and many passengers, to port, we struck bad weather and, in the storm, my ship hit a huge rock. The rock tore a hole out of the hulk and the water began to rush in and I knew that we were going to sink. All the passengers crowded onto the deck, weeping and praying. They knew we were lost. There was no help for us. And in their despair they cried out to me that if there were some way the ship could be saved, they would give one-third of the cargo to the man who would save them."

"Yes, yes," Solomon cried, jumping to his feet. "Then what happened?"

The captain swung around to him. "I don't quite know what happened, Your Highness. I knew there was nothing *I* could do to save the ship, and I was engaged in praying, along with the passengers, when suddenly a sharp and strong wind came blowing over the ship, and . . . perhaps you won't believe me?"

"Go on, go on," King David and Solomon cried together.

"I know it sounds unlikely . . ." the captain hesitated.

"Go on, go on," Solomon and King David shouted.

"Well, it seemed to me that the wind was carrying a sack of flour, almost as if the wind had hands!" He stopped and waited, but when neither the King nor the Prince laughed or ridiculed him, he continued. "And it seemed to me as if the fingers of the wind opened the sack and spread the flour out evenly all along the cracks where the water was rushing into the boat, and the flour stuck together like paste and stopped the leaks. The boat stopped sinking, and we were saved!"

Solomon and his father looked at each other and laughed. And then, quickly, Solomon, receiving permission from his father by a brief nod, told the captain the story of Caleb and how his sack of flour was carried out to sea, and how Solomon had summoned the West Wind who had told him that he had taken that sack of flour to save the captain's ship. When Solomon finished, the captain cried,

"I must find this Caleb! His reward is waiting for him."

"Wait!" King David commanded. "We shall go with you."

He ordered his chariot, and he and Solomon rode in the chariot, followed by the captain who rode in a wagon which he had left outside the palace gate. They took the sea road and soon came to the humble little home of Caleb. As the chariot of the King stopped in front of the door, Deborah, the oldest daughter came running out.

When she saw the splendid chariot, she gasped, "Oh!"

"Little girl," King David said. "Is your father home?"

"Oh yes, sir," Deborah said, curtsying.

She ran indoors calling, "Father, father!"

In a moment, Caleb, followed by all three little girls, came hurrying out of the house.

"The King!" Caleb exclaimed. "The King does great honor to the house of Caleb!" he cried and bowed low.

All the little girls curtsied, peeking at young Solomon through their eyelashes. The youngest girls giggled and hid behind their father. But Deborah stood quietly, waiting, her eyes shining.

"Caleb," King David said as the captain walked forward from his wagon. "Here is the captain of the ship which you saved."

"I saved!" Caleb exclaimed. "Your Majesty, please forgive me. I don't understand what you are saying . . ."

"Father, let me tell," cried young Solomon, watching the pretty Deborah.

Then the young prince told Caleb and Deborah the story of what the West Wind had told him, and of what the captain had reported — how the sack of flour which belonged to Caleb had saved the ship and the cargo and the passengers.

Then the captain spoke up.

"And sir," he said to Caleb. "My passengers insist on paying one-third of the cargo to the man who was responsible for saving our ship and our lives.

In that wagon, you will find one-third of the cargo. It is all yours, sir, all yours."

King David led the way to the wagon, followed by young Solomon, with the captain behind him, and Caleb and Deborah, unbelieving and astonished, following the captain, with the two younger girls running ahead, squealing and giggling. And there in the wagon they saw spices and silver and precious cloth!

"And it is all mine!" Caleb exclaimed.

"It is all yours," Solomon said. "Now you have riches enough to take care of your three pretty daughters."

Thus did the wind which blew the sack of flour out to the sea, blow good fortune to Caleb and his three little daughters.

The Serpent At Court

While still a young boy, Solomon enjoyed sitting in his father's court, listening to all cases brought before the King. David was pleased at Solomon's interest and, indeed, he frequently depended on his judgment. None of David's other sons cared about what they called "dry lawsuits." Absalom was too busy trying to start a rebellion against his father. Adonijah was occupied riding around in his chariot, with men running before him shouting, "Make way for the King." Chileab, though a scholar, was too shy to speak up before people. He frequently attended the court but lost himself in the crowd so no one would point him out as the King's son. And Amnon cared only for pleasure. To sit in a courtroom all day to him was too dreary. He wanted fun.

But Solomon found it enjoyable to sit in his father's courtroom because every case was different and presented interesting problems. Many of the cases involved sorrows, or troubles, or tragedies. Once in a while there was a dramatic situation, or even a humorous incident. Such a case came before the King one cold winter morning.

In Jerusalem there lived a man named Johanan. He was called a physician by some, and he actually was a doctor, not of people but of animals. He loved animals so much that it hurt him if they were in pain and he could never rest until he cured them.

On this cold winter morning he was returning from the home of a farmer-friend whose sheep had been stricken with a serious illness. Johanan had spent all night in the sheepcote and left only when he knew the sheep were out of danger. As he neared the town, he heard an animal whimpering in pain with an almost human voice. He looked all around, but could see nothing near him. He called out,

"Who weeps? And where are you?"

A voice answered him, "I weep, here, near this tree."

Johanan went close to the tree and there, half-coiled, lay a serpent.

"O friend Serpent," Johanan exclaimed. "Why do you weep so bitterly?"

"Because I'm cold," wailed the Serpent. "I'm frozen. Any moment I shall freeze to death."

"What a pity," Johanan said. "I'll help you. Don't worry. I'll save your life. I'll warm you. Let's see, what can I cover you with?"

He looked all around, but there was nothing he could use as a blanket. The earth was frozen hard. The leaves were crushed into dust.

"You said you'd help me," whined the Serpent. "But see, you do nothing but stand there and shake your head."

"Patience, Serpent, patience," Johanan said. "I'm trying to find you a cover."

"That's a nice warm coat *you're* wearing," the Serpent said slyly.

31

"Oh yes," Johanan said. "But if I give you my coat, I shall freeze. But then, I'll tell you what, friend Serpent. We'll share my coat."

"Good, oh good," the Serpent said.

Johanan unbuttoned his coat, picked up the Serpent and put him inside the coat. The Serpent lay next to Johanan's body, absorbing its warmth. After a minute, he murmured,

"Good, oh good. I feel better already."

"Fine." Johanan smiled, glad to be helping so quickly and so well.

But, in the next moment, suddenly, without warning, the Serpent coiled itself around Johanan's ribs and started squeezing.

"Here, here," admonished Johanan. "You're hurting me. Look out there, friend, or you'll squeeze me to death."

"That's exactly what I aim to do," hissed the Serpent. "I'm going to squeeze you to death."

"Here now, that's very unfriendly," Johanan said, turning pale, feeling that it was getting hard for him to breathe.

"Unfriendly, am I?" sneered the Serpent, squeezing a little harder on Johanan's ribs.

"Yes," Johanan said staunchly. "Unfriendly and unfair. I have saved your life and, instead of so much as saying 'Thank you,' you're trying to take my life. Now why?"

The Serpent hissed and squeezed a little harder. Johanan was panting for breath. The Serpent said,

"I just don't like men, that's why. I have you in my power and I'm going to squeeze you to death."

"Well, I most certainly protest," Johanan said sternly. "I have never hurt you or any of your animal friends. In fact, whenever they're sick, I'm the first to help them. Is this my reward?"

"I don't care," hissed the Serpent, "how you help other animals. I just don't like men and you're a man, so I shall kill you."

"Wait!" cried Johanan, feeling his breath coming harder and harder. "I say that you have no right to kill me."

"Oh yes, I have," said the Serpent. "Man is the enemy of the Serpent."

"But I say it is unjust," Johanan said. "Let us go to court and see whose case is more just, yours or mine."

The Serpent thought this over. Then he said,

"Very well, I agree. Let us ask the first thing we meet."

He loosened his hold on Johanan slightly, and Johanan breathed more easily. He began to walk very fast, and the Serpent grumbled,

"Hey there, not so fast. You're jiggling me."

Johanan slowed up a trifle. He walked for ten agonizing minutes, fearful that the Serpent at any moment would break his promise and simply crush him to death. At the end of ten minutes, they met an Ox.

"Here, stop here," said the Serpent. "Let's put our case before the Ox."

"The Ox!" exclaimed Johanan. "Why, he's just a work animal. He doesn't know the difference between right and wrong."

"Ask the Ox," threatened the Serpent. "Or I'll crush you to death right here."

Johanan stopped. The Serpent poked his head out of the coat and hissed,

"Ho there, friend Ox. A moment of your time, if you please."

"One moment, just one moment," the Ox said gloomily. "I have no more to spare than that. I must get on with my work."

"Just one moment is all I ask," the Serpent said. "Hear me, friend Ox. I was lying on the ground, freezing to death. This man came along . . ."

"And saved his life," Johanan burst in, "by putting him inside my coat. And to reward me, he says he will squeeze me to death."

"I'm right to do so," the Serpent said. "Man is my enemy. What think you, friend Ox?"

"Aye, aye," lowed the Ox gloomily. "Such is the way of the world. Oh these men. Listen to me, Serpent, you do right to kill him. Yes, I know these men. I hate them too."

"Is that gratitude?" Johanan cried. "Your master feeds you and gives you a warm barn . . ."

The Ox interrupted. "Listen to my side of the story. My master works me hard, oh, very, very hard. And with what result? He takes the best of the food; and what does he give me? Oh, nothing but oats and straw and a little brackish water to wash it down. Oh yes, my master works me hard, oh very, very hard. And with what result? He takes the softest bed to sleep in, but I am left outdoors in the blinding sun, in the chilling rain, in the freezing winds and snows. Yes, yes, friend Serpent. Kill the man. That's what I say."

And the Ox turned and lumbered away.

"Hee, hee, I'm right," hissed the Serpent, tightening his squeezing hold on the man.

"Wait, wait," cried Johanan. "The Ox was a prejudiced witness. Let's ask another."

"Oh, very well," the Serpent agreed matter-of-factly. "I don't care if I kill you now or an hour from now."

Johanan started walking again hurriedly. And soon they met a Donkey.

"Ho there, friend Donkey," greeted the Serpent. "Stop. We want your advice."

"For nothing?" brayed the Donkey.

"Do you have a carrot?" the Serpent asked Johanan.

"Why yes, I do happen to have a carrot in my pocket. I always carry one, in case I meet a hungry animal."

"Less talking, please," the Donkey said. "And hand over that carrot."

"You're a bit rude," Johanan said, pulling the carrot out of his pocket and putting it into the Donkey's mouth.

"So would you be, if you were a donkey," said the Donkey, and began to chew on the carrot. "What's your problem?" he asked the Serpent.

"I want to know if it's right for me to kill this man," the Serpent said.

"Sure, sure." The Donkey nodded, his long ears flapping, and he chewed away on the carrot.

"But I've just saved his life," Johanan cried.

34

"Small difference," the Donkey said carelessly.

A piece of carrot lodged in his throat and he began to bray. When he coughed it up, he said,

"You see how cruel men are? You gave me the carrot so I would choke to death. Certainly, friend Serpent, you should kill the man. Man's always trying to kill me with hard work. He piles heavier and heavier loads on me, and he keeps the choice food for himself and gives me straw to eat. At the end of a hard day, does he give me a soft bed to lie in? Oh no. He keeps the soft bed for himself and leaves me to sleep out in the frost and miserable drizzle. Yes, yes, kill the man. Kill him."

And the Donkey turned and plodded away.

"Aha," the Serpent wiggled happily, "Good advice."

He began to squeeze again on Johanan's ribs.

"Just a moment," Johanan said angrily. "I never saw a more prejudiced witness. And I even gave him a carrot."

"That's what comes from bribing a witness," the Serpent said and laughed.

"Bribing!" Johanan exclaimed. "You told me to give him the carrot. So I didn't attempt to bribe the witness at all. And now see here, I'm tired of all this fooling around. I propose that we go to a real court-of-law. Let us go to King David's court."

"Will his son Solomon be there?" asked the Serpent.

"I suppose so," Johanan said. "What difference does that make?"

"Oh, Solomon likes animals," answered the Serpent. "He talks our language. He'll decide in my favor, never fear. Get along there, O man. On your way."

"Keep a civil tongue in your head," Johanan said angrily and started off almost at a run.

When they reached the court and registered with the Court Recorder, they had to wait almost an hour for their case to be called. Many people looked curiously at Johanan because he didn't remove his heavy coat in the warm room. Besides, loud hissing sounds were coming from his direction and people kept saying, "Sh, sh." Between the hissing of the Serpent which embarrassed him, and the heaviness of his outer coat which made him uncomfortable, Johanan spent a miserable hour.

Finally the Court Recorder called,

"Hear ye. Hear ye. Next case. Case number 6 Aleph 321, the case of Johanan and the Serpent."

"Serpent!"

The word echoed through the room. Everyone craned his neck to look. So that's where the hissing came from! But, where was the Serpent?

Johanan, his face red with embarrassment, approached the throne. He bowed stiffly, as best he could with the Serpent coiled around him.

"Your Majesty," he said to King David. And to young Solomon, "Your Highness."

"State your case," King David said kindly.

Johanan unbuttoned his coat, took it off, and everyone in the room gasped to see the Serpent coiled tightly around his ribs.

"What have we here?" King David asked sharply.

"Your Majesty," Johanan said quickly. "This morning as I was walking along the road, I came upon this Serpent whimpering piteously. He said he was freezing to death. So I put him under my coat to warm him up and thereby, Your Majesty, I saved his life. But, instead of being grateful to me, suddenly he coiled himself around me and has been threatening to crush me to death. Now, Your Majesty, I appeal for justice."

"And so do I!" hissed the Serpent.

"Your Majesty," Johanan pleaded. "Do I deserve death for saving the Serpent's life?"

"Is this story the truth?" King David asked the Serpent.

"Oh yes," the Serpent admitted readily. "I was freezing. He did save my life. But I hate men. I have hated men ever since the days of the Garden of Eden when the first Serpent was punished because man was foolish enough to eat the forbidden fruit."

"But it was the Serpent who persuaded man to sin," King David said. "And so the Serpent had to be punished."

"Well," said the Serpent, "Man shouldn't have listened and the first Serpent shouldn't have been punished. So I hate men and now I have this one in my power."

King David looked sternly at Johanan. "You know the Serpent is man's enemy. You should have killed him when you had him in your power."

"That's unfair, Your Majesty," cried the Serpent. Then he laughed. "But it's too late now. I have him in *my* power."

Young Solomon spoke up. "Father, may I speak?"

"Yes, my son," King David said. "Speak."

Young Solomon addressed the Serpent. "Hear me, O Serpent. In a court-

36

of-law, it is required that both sides of a case must enjoy the same advantage."

"Yes, Your Highness," the Serpent answered.

"Just now you have the advantage over the man," Solomon said. "And that is so unfair that we cannot go on with this case. Uncoil yourself. Release the man. Get down to the floor. Then we shall continue the case."

"But, Your Highness," whined the Serpent. "I don't want to loosen my hold on him."

"Get to the floor," Solomon ordered. "Or we shall not go on with your case."

"You're certainly asking too much of me," the Serpent whimpered, loosening his hold.

He began to uncoil, and slithered down along Johanan's leg and then, reaching the floor, coiled up and said,

"There you are, Your Highness. Now let us proceed with the case."

"Now both parties are equal before the court," Solomon said. He turned to Johanan. "My noble father was right. You should have killed the Serpent. He is your enemy."

"I've been tricked," shrieked the Serpent from the floor.

"Less than you tried to trick this man," Solomon said. "You repaid his kindness with treachery. For that you should die. I should order this man to kill you."

"No, no," shrieked the Serpent. "Oh, I've been tricked, tricked."

"Silence," ordered Solomon. "You're hardly in a position to complain of trickery. Now hear me, O Serpent. And hear me, O man. Justice demands that for his deceit and for his treachery, the Serpent should die."

"No, no," wailed the Serpent, coiling and uncoiling on the floor.

"But this court," Solomon said, "tempers justice with mercy. And so we shall let you live, Serpent. Go now. Go free, and live, but don't you ever again act so treacherously. Go!"

The Serpent, wailing and hissing, coiled along the floor, out of the door, back to the fields.

Johanan was saved.

King David and his court congratulated young Solomon on his clever handling of the case, and repeated over and over the words,

"Justice must be tempered with mercy," even to a serpent.

The Wheatfield On Mount Zion

When old King David died, young Solomon ascended the throne. Before he could undertake any new projects as the new king, he had to clear up many old affairs left over from his father's administration. His brother Absalom had been killed in the rebellion he had led against David. Amnon had died long before. Adonijah had to be handled sternly, so that he would not rebel against his younger brother. Chileab, the studious brother, was put in charge of a new school and he liked that better than sitting on a throne and wearing a crown. Now the kingdom was secure against internal strife.

The next thing Solomon did was to build a magnificent tomb for his father.

And then he was ready to undertake a new and very important task. He summoned his most trusted lieutenant, Benaiah, to his audience chamber. When Benaiah arrived, he found King Solomon engaged in conversation with the captain of a vessel which was ready to depart for far-away eastern lands.

"Remember," King Solomon was saying to the captain. "Be sure to go to Ophir. In Ophir you will purchase finely-spun gold. It can only be found in that land."

He finished giving his orders to the captain and dismissed him. Then he explained to Benaiah,

"That fine-spun gold is what I shall use to build my new throne."

Benaiah smiled. "Your Majesty, are you going to build the throne before you build your new palace?"

"No," Solomon answered. "I am not going to build the throne before I build the palace. And I am not going to build the palace before I build . . ."

The King stopped. Benaiah leaned forward.

"Yes?" he prompted the King. "Yes, Your Majesty? Before you build what?"

"Before I build the Temple."

Benaiah smiled. "Good. It is right to build the Temple first. Where will you build it?"

"That I have not yet decided," King Solomon said. "You and I are going now to search for the best place in Jerusalem on which to build the Temple."

He gave orders for his chariot to be made ready. Then he and Benaiah went forth into the city. They went up into the hills and down into the valleys but nowhere did they find the place that seemed suitable. One place was too shallow and another place was too small and a third place seemed too insignificant.

They searched the whole afternoon, and then King Solomon turned the chariot about and they returned to the palace. It was almost time for the evening meal. The King felt weary and decided to take a little rest before eating. At the door of his bedroom as he parted from Benaiah, he said,

"Tomorrow morning we shall go out and search again."

He went into the bedroom, flung himself on a couch and in one minute was sound asleep. It was a very short sleep the King had, perhaps not more than five minutes. But he awoke greatly refreshed from this nap because he had had a wonderful dream.

It seemed to him as if in his sleep he had heard a heavenly voice proclaim to him:

> "Solomon, go thou to Mount Zion. Find thou the wheatfield
> owned by two brothers. Seek there and see if thou canst find
> the site for the Temple."

When Solomon awoke, the voice of his dream seemed still to be uttering its clear words:

> "Go thou to Mount Zion."

He opened his door and shouted, "Benaiah! Benaiah!"

Benaiah came running and found the King changing from his rumpled clothes into clean garments.

"Benaiah," he shouted. "We shall not wait for the morning. I know now where to search for a site for the Temple. I fell asleep and I dreamed, and in my dream I heard a voice and the voice said, 'Go thou to Mount Zion.' Let us eat, Benaiah. Then we shall go."

The King and Benaiah ate their evening meal hurriedly. But, important as their errand was, and eagerly as Solomon wanted to set out on his search, yet, since there was still some daylight left, they took time for their regular evening game of chess. But this time neither Benaiah nor the King could keep his mind on the game. Of course, as usual, the King won. And, as he said, "Checkmate," Benaiah, looking out through the window, answered,

"I see the stars. The darkness has come."

"Then let us go," Solomon said.

"But how will you find the place in the darkness?"

"Never fear," the King answered, "I shall find it."

They left the palace and, riding in the chariot, went directly to Mount Zion. At the foot of the mountain they dismounted and, with the moon to guide them, began the long climb upwards. Wherever they saw what looked like a wheatfield growing on the mountainside, they stopped, only to discover that it was a field of clover or a field of oats. And so they climbed higher and higher until they reached the mountain top.

There, clearly revealed in the moonlight, stretched a large field of wheat. At one end of the field was a big, white house. At the farthest end of the field was a poor, little hut. Dividing the field in two, running the whole length of it, was a low stone fence, gleaming white in the moonlight.

Solomon and Benaiah, about to go forward, were stopped by movement near the stone fence. They strained their eyes to see through the darkness

40

and they saw two men, one on each side of the stone fence, harvesting wheat.

"What are those two men doing?" King Solomon asked.

"This is harvesting time," Benaiah answered.

"But since when do our farmers harvest during the night?"

Benaiah shrugged. "Perhaps on the top of the mountain, that is considered the best hour. I admit, it's the first time I've seen harvesting done at night."

For a few moments they watched in silence and then they saw something even stranger than men harvesting at night. They saw one man, on the east side of the field, lifting huge armfuls of wheat and dropping them over the stone fence. Then they saw the other man, on the west side of the fence, lifting huge armfuls of wheat and dropping them over the other side.

"This looks strange," the King said. "Why does one man drop his wheat over the fence into the other's field, while the other drops his wheat over the fence into the first man's field! There is some mystery here. Let us see."

With that they strode forward talking in normal voices so that the men would hear them come and not mistake them for thieves.

"Hello there," the King called out as they came near the spot where they had seen the two men.

No one answered and now, in the dark night, there was no one to be seen.

"Hello there," the King called again. "I am the King, King Solomon. Hello there, I say."

At that, the man on the west side of the stone fence rose from the ground where he had stooped to hide on hearing their voices. He bowed and said,

"Welcome, O King, to my poor field of wheat."

The man on the east side of the stone fence, hearing that the conversation was all friendly, likewise rose, and bowed and said,

"Welcome, O King, to my poor field of wheat."

"Greetings," King Solomon said. "My lieutenant and I were standing over there," he pointed back to the crest of the mountain, "and we saw something which looked peculiar to us. You, sir," he said to the man on the west side of the fence, "gathered wheat and dropped it over the stone wall; and you," he said to the other man, "did likewise. Why do you drop your wheat onto each other's fields?"

The two men turned to look at each other through the darkness, and then they both began to laugh.

"Oh, Your Majesty," the man on the east said. "Forgive our unseemly laughter, and let me explain what has been happening." He chuckled once more, and said, "This man and I are brothers. People call me the rich brother because I have some wealth and also a large family: I have seven children."

"And people call me the poor brother," the man on the west said, "because I have no money and because I have no children at all."

"Now is the time of the harvest," the rich brother continued. "I decided to do my harvesting at night when my brother could not see so that I could add some of the harvest from my own field to his wheat, since he is poor and I thought he could use the extra wheat."

The poor brother laughed. "I, too, decided to do my harvesting in the nighttime because I thought that my brother, even though he is rich, could use some of my wheat since he has so many children to feed, and that is why I dropped some over onto his field."

The two brothers laughed together and put their arms around each other's shoulders. King Solomon and Benaiah looked at each other and nodded even though it was dark and they could hardly see each other. But just then the moon came out from behind a cloud and lit up the faces of the four men.

King Solomon spoke. "I once heard my father say when he was composing one of his psalms, 'Behold, how good and how pleasant it is when brothers dwell together in friendship.' This is a wonderful example of brotherly love. Each of you has tried to help the other without being asked. And because there was so much genuine affection shown here in this field of wheat, this place seems holy to me. I believe it would be just the right place to build the Temple."

"The Temple?" exclaimed the rich brother. "Ah, how wonderful it would be to have the Temple built here on our wheatfield."

"Here?" said the poor brother. "What could be a better gift to God? I gladly give you my half of the wheatfield on which to build the Temple."

"No, no," King Solomon said. "I do not mean to ask you for a gift of this wheatfield. It is enough that your brotherly love has pointed out the proper place to me. I shall buy the field from you."

"Then you will both be rich," Benaiah said, smiling.

"And here," King Solomon said, "on the top of Mount Zion where we have seen such fine brotherly love, where two brothers have worked together in friendship, we shall build the Temple where all men shall learn to live together as brothers."

The Capture of Asmodeus

After that dark night when King Solomon and his lieutenant Benaiah found the site for the Temple on Mount Zion, some peculiar things started to happen to Benaiah. Whenever he was about to eat any food, it was snatched away from him and vanished into thin air. Whenever he was about to put any money into his pouch, it was pulled out of his hand and it too vanished into thin air. This happened to him one day, two days, three days, and then he complained to the King about it.

The King listened carefully and then he said,

"This must be the work of a demon. I shall have to capture that sprite and see what this mischief's about."

He laid one trap after another, but he could not succeed in catching hold of the demon. And poor Benaiah was getting very, very hungry indeed. Then Solomon prayed to God for help in conquering this mischievous sprite.

That evening, as Solomon slept, the Archangel Michael appeared in his dream and spoke to him.

"On your pillow, O Solomon, I am placing a small ring. This ring has a seal on it consisting of an engraved stone. This is a gift to you, Solomon, the King, the son of David, from the Lord on high. With the help of this ring, O Solomon, you shall capture and bind up all the demons and you shall use their strength and skill to help build the Temple. Take good care of this ring, O Solomon. It gives you great power."

Michael's voice drifted away. The dream faded. The King awoke. And there, on his pillow, was a small ring, with a seal consisting of an engraved stone!

He sat up, picked up the ring, rubbed it and said,

"Demon, Demon, appear before me. Demon, Demon, appear before Solomon. Demon, Demon, appear before the King."

Suddenly a blue light glowed at the foot of the bed. Out of the blue light stepped a small creature dressed all in blue.

"You have summoned me, O Solomon. You have summoned me, O King."

"Who are you?" Solomon demanded. "What is your name?"

"I am Ornias, Your Majesty. At your service."

"Are you the demon who has been plaguing my lieutenant Benaiah," asked the King.

"I am," Ornias said.

"Why do you snatch the food from my good lieutenant?" Solomon asked. "Why do you steal his money?"

Ornias shrugged slightly, smiled impudently, and said,

"Oh, I was just having a little fun."

"Fun," said the King. "So all you think of is fun. It's clear you have too much time on your hands. Idleness breeds mischief. I shall have to put you to work."

Ornias twisted and turned, trying to escape, but when he found he couldn't move from that spot, he whined,

"I like to play, Your Majesty. I don't like to work."

"But work you shall," King Solomon said. "Here, now, gaze upon this seal, and with the memory of it in your eye, fetch for me ten thousand demons, healthy and strong. I am going to build a Temple to the Lord and the demons are going to work to quarry the stones and do other hard labor and, for once, they will be out of mischief and doing something useful."

Ornias gazed upon the ring. And then he was completely in the King's power. He bowed, and said meekly,

"I go at your command, O King, but I tell you again, I'd rather play than work."

The blue light faded away. The sprite was gone. King Solomon went back to sleep.

Ornias went to fulfill the royal command. He did not dare go directly to the king of the demons, Asmodeus. Instead he went to Asmodeus' lieutenant, Beelzebul, and gave him Solomon's message. Beelzebul promised to bring the ten thousand demons to the King to work in the quarries.

And he did. He brought the Demon of the Ashes, Tephros, and his seven helpers, and Solomon set them to work carrying away the dirt from the foundation of the Temple. Ornias was given the task of carrying the water to the building site. And to a demon called Rabdos was given the task of cutting the stone from the quarries. But Rabdos did not go to work as the others did. He just sat around and grumbled; and when the foreman of the construction job complained to the King, he summoned Rabdos.

"Why do you not cut the stone from the quarries as I have commanded?" the King asked.

"Because, Your Majesty," Rabdos said meekly. "I have no tools. You know well, O King, that I cannot dig out the stone with my fingernails. I need a hammer and a pickax and a number of other tools."

"Those tools you cannot have," Solomon said. "We are prohibited from using iron tools in making the altar. You will have to use your hands."

"I cannot do that, Your Majesty," Rabdos said pitifully. "O wise King, you know I cannot quarry stone with my hands."

The King, knowing of course that no one, not even a demon, could quarry stone with his bare fingers, dismissed him. Then he called together the scholars of the realm and put his problem before them. How could the stones be cut from the quarry if they were not permitted to use tools made of iron?

The scholars argued the question to and fro but all agreed on one thing, that it *was* prohibited to use iron tools in making the altar.

Finally Solomon said impatiently, "You've spent many hours stating the case as I know it to be. Now solve the problem for me."

"If the wise King Solomon doesn't know the answer . . ." The President of the Sanhedrin smiled and shrugged his shoulders.

Then one scholar spoke up.

"Your Majesty, I remember that when Moses wished to engrave the names of the twelve tribes on the ephod of the High Priest, he used a worm, but I cannot remember what worm . . ."

"I remember," cried out another scholar. "It's a worm called the Shamir. It cuts rocks. It cuts the hardest stone. Yes, yes, I remember. It is the Shamir."

"Where can I find the Shamir worm?" King Solomon asked.

"That I do not know," the second scholar said.

"Nor I," said the first.

Solomon looked from one scholar to another, but they all shook their heads. No one knew where the Shamir could be found. When the King saw that he could get no further help from them, he thanked them for coming and dismissed them.

Then he summoned the leaders of the demons. Ornias came and Beelzebul, Tephros and Rabdos. They bowed, waiting for him to speak. The King said,

"I have discovered that there is a worm which can split rocks. It is called the Shamir. Where will I find it?"

"Your Majesty," Ornias said. "I regret, I do not know."

"Beelzebul?" the King asked.

But Beelzebul shook his head, and Tephros shook his head. They did not know. Then Rabdos spoke up.

"If any one knows, O King, it will be Asmodeus, our demon-king."

"Asmodeus is king of the demons?" Solomon exclaimed. "Why was he not brought to me before this?"

They all shook their heads and Ornias said, "O King, O Solomon, Asmodeus is the *king* of the demons. He is more powerful than any of us. We could never capture him for you."

"You cannot or will not?" Solomon asked.

Tephros looked as frightened as a demon can look and said weakly, "We cannot, Your Majesty, and we would not, Your Majesty. He would punish us severely."

"Then I shall get him myself," Solomon said. "I must have Asmodeus. I shall have Asmodeus."

The demons began to back away.

"Halt!" Solomon commanded. "At least you can tell me this. Where shall I find him?"

Tephros kept silent. So did Rabdos and Ornias. Then Beelzebul said, "Your Majesty, I shall tell you where to find him."

And then he told the King the name of the mountain on which Asmodeus lived. And Rabdos said,

"On this mountain there is a well from which Asmodeus drinks every evening. In the morning he closes it with a large rock which he seals. In the evening, when he returns, he examines the seal to see that the well has not been tampered with, removes the seal, and then he drinks from that well."

Armed with this knowledge, Solomon gave Benaiah the task of bringing Asmodeus, the king of the demons, to him.

Benaiah exclaimed aloud. "Your Majesty! I, bring the king of the demons! Oh your Majesty! I know that people call me a hero. But I am only a mortal man. Why, Solomon, my King, you know Asmodeus would bewitch me or kill me before I could so much as get near him!"

"I have a plan," Solomon said. "Listen."

And he whispered long into Benaiah's ear. Then he gave him his magic ring, a chain, a bundle of wool and a flask of wine. Benaiah left on this hazardous task after saying good-bye to everyone he knew, feeling sure he would never return. But the King had ordered him to go, so he went.

He travelled for a long time until he came to the mountain where, he was told, the king of the demons, Asmodeus, came to drink. It was just about noontime when Benaiah arrived and, after searching about on the side of a hill, he found the well which was covered with a stone and sealed with a strange seal, and he knew that this was the well from which Asmodeus drew his drinking water.

Benaiah set quickly to work. He dug a hole on the lower side of the hill to let the water out. Then he stuffed up the hole with part of the wool that he brought with him. Then higher up on the hill he dug another hole through which he let in the wine that he had brought, and that hole he stuffed too with some wool. In this way, through the clever scheme which had been worked out by King Solomon, he substituted wine for water in Asmodeus' well without disturbing the seal.

Satisfied that all was well, he searched around for a high bush behind which he could conceal himself. There he rested, eating his noon-day meal, taking a nap for an hour. As the afternoon began to wane and the time drew near for Asmodeus to appear, Benaiah roused himself to full wakefulness and complete watchfulness.

After a while Benaiah heard a clanking and a grunting and a hoarse voice singing. He peeped through the leaves of the bushes and saw, coming towards the well, a fierce-looking demon. It was Asmodeus. He went directly to the well. He examined the seal and saw that it was in perfect condition. It looked as if no one had tampered with it. So he removed the seal and from his belt took a cup and with it he drew up a cupful of water. What was his astonishment to find that it was not water, but wine! He threw it to the ground. He would drink no wine!

He prowled around the well, trying to decide what had happened. Who had tricked him, and why? But he could find no evidence of anyone's having been there. Benaiah watched from behind the thick bush, waiting for Asmodeus to drink the wine. But Asmodeus growled and muttered and stalked round and round the well, refusing to touch the wine. But as minute followed minute, he became thirstier and thirstier.

Finally he said aloud,

"I cannot see any sign of anyone's having tampered with this well. And I am so thirsty I cannot bear it. I must drink something. So I shall drink one little mouthful of this wine. That won't hurt me."

He drew up a cupful of the wine from the well and sipped at it, but he was so very thirsty that just sipping didn't help, so he gulped down the whole cup of wine. The wine, being sweet, only made him thirstier, so he drew up

another cupful of wine, and drank it, and then another cupful, and another, another, until finally the wine overpowered him and he fell sound asleep.

Benaiah waited for a long time, and then waited again, to make certain that the dangerous Asmodeus was really and truly asleep. Then, very cautiously, he crawled out from behind the thick bush, and walked carefully and noiselessly over to the sleeping Asmodeus. Quickly he slipped the chain around the neck of the king of the demons.

And, he had captured Asmodeus!

As the chain rubbed against Asmodeus' neck, he awoke. His eyes were heavy from sleep. He rubbed them, then grunted, pulling on the chain around his neck. He looked up, and there towering over him, was Benaiah.

"Who are you?" Asmodeus roared. "And what do you to me?"

"I am Benaiah, the servant of Solomon, the King. And I have captured you for him."

"Never!" shouted Asmodeus. "Release me. Release me, I say. I am the king of the demons!"

"You are not a king now," Benaiah said. "You are a captive of the King whose name is Solomon. You are in his power. Come along with me."

"I shall cast a spell over you," shouted Asmodeus. "Release me or I shall bewitch you."

"Cease your idle boasts," Benaiah said. "You have no power over me. I wear the magic ring of King Solomon. Come along now."

And Asmodeus, the king of the demons, as meekly as a little lamb, followed Benaiah down the mountainside towards Jerusalem.

The Demon's Strange Behavior

Asmodeus, the great king of the demons, was captured by Benaiah, King Solomon's lieutenant. Benaiah had used great cunning in outwitting the demon. Asmodeus had thought this could never happen to him and he raged in fury. But finally he stopped struggling.

Then Benaiah led him along on the end of the chain with which he had been captured, down the steep mountain slopes, through a valley until they reached a little village. As they began walking through this village, they came to a grove of palm trees. Benaiah tried to walk in the middle of the road, but Asmodeus pulled him over closer and closer to the trees. He wanted to terrify Benaiah by showing him how strong he was. So as they came up to a very tall and strong palm tree, Asmodeus brushed against it. It began to topple, its upper branches creaking as it fell, and then it crashed, uprooted from the ground!

Asmodeus began to walk quietly on, leading the way back to the center of the road.

But Benaiah stopped. In surprise, he said, "Now why did you uproot that palm tree?"

Asmodeus growled at him, and said, "It is enough that you have captured me. I don't have to tell you my secrets too."

He started to walk on haughtily. Benaiah shrugged, and on they went through the village, until they reached a large forest. Benaiah led the way through the underbrush, over stones and through narrow paths until they came out of the forest into another village, larger than the last one they had come through.

Soon they met a small, thin man who stumbled across their path.

"Ho, look where you're going," Asmodeus shouted to the man.

"I can't," the man answered. "I am blind and I have lost my way."

"Where do you want to go?" Asmodeus asked.

"To the well in the center of the city," the blind man answered.

Asmodeus grasped hold of the man's arm, turned him to the right, and said, "There, the path is under your feet now. Just keep walking on this path."

"Thank you, sir," the blind man said, walking off.

Before Benaiah could say, "Now why did you do that?" Asmodeus looked at him, and grinned, and Benaiah held his tongue. And on they continued until suddenly a big, strong man, with his hair falling over his eyes, lurched right in front of them.

"Ho, this man is drunk," Asmodeus said, grasping the man by the arms. "I think he wants to find a soft place to lie down and sleep."

He turned the man around and gave him a little shove towards the village park.

"Now why . . ." Benaiah started to say.

But Asmodeus interrupted. "I don't have to tell you my secrets."

They continued on through the village until they came to a river. Here they walked along the shore until they found a footpath of wide flat stones. Benaiah made Asmodeus go first so that he wouldn't pull any tricks and try to topple him off into the water to drown. They reached the other side safely, and found themselves in a still larger village.

"Now, no uprooting of trees or knocking over houses," Benaiah warned Asmodeus. "Behave yourself."

"Oh, I don't want to uproot any trees," Asmodeus said, and laughed. "And why should I knock over any houses?"

Benaiah scowled at him, and on they walked until suddenly they heard the sound of music. From around a bend in the road came a wedding party, the bride and groom leading the way and the rest of the guests walking behind, laughing and talking, everyone acting gay and happy.

But, as the wedding party passed them, Asmodeus broke into loud wailing. He sobbed and wept until the wedding party had passed by them, looking back over their shoulders, annoyed and astonished at this peculiar behavior.

When they were out of earshot, Benaiah said, angrily,

"Now why did you spoil that wedding joy with your false weeping?"

Asmodeus pulled at the chain around his throat, and said,

"Come, come, we're wasting time. And to you I do not tell my secrets."

By that time they were almost at the door of a shoemaker's shop. Standing at the door was a big, strong man who was saying to the shoemaker,

"Make me a pair of strong shoes. Make me a pair of shoes which will last for seven years."

Asmodeus burst out laughing. The shoemaker looked up in surprise. The man looked at him huffily and strode away, and Benaiah pulled Asmodeus away from the shop, saying angrily,

"Now that was a stupid thing to do, to laugh at that man. You probably hurt his feelings. Why shouldn't he want a pair of shoes that will last seven years?"

"No secrets," Asmodeus said gleefully. "You'll get no secrets out of me!"

Just before they left this town, they came upon a group of people. In the center stood a magician showing his tricks of magic. They were very good tricks and Benaiah, who always liked magic, wanted to see them. Asmodeus, though he knew so many tricks of his own, always liked to learn new ones. So they stopped to watch.

The magician was very clever and he did one good trick after another. All the people and Benaiah stood in wonder, eyes staring, open-mouthed. But Asmodeus began to smile. Then he giggled. Then he chuckled. And then he began to laugh out loud. And he laughed and laughed, so hard and so long that the magician had to stop his show. The people glared at Asmodeus for spoiling their fun. Benaiah said,

"Here, here. Stop that."

But Asmodeus laughed and laughed until Benaiah, in disgust, yanked at Asmodeus's chain and pulled him away. Of course there was no use asking why he had laughed. Benaiah knew, by now, that he wouldn't tell him. So in silence they continued their journey.

They travelled on and on until finally they reached Jerusalem, and the palace. Benaiah handed his prisoner over to the Warden of the Royal Prison and went to see Solomon.

"Did you get Asmodeus?" Solomon asked eagerly.

"Oh yes, I got him," Benaiah answered wearily.

"He must have put up a strong struggle," the King said. "You look exhausted."

"Oh, I am exhausted," Benaiah said. "But not from any struggle. Asmodeus did try to best me, but I had your magic ring." He handed the ring to the King. "I captured him easily enough. But it was our journey which wearied me so."

54

"What is there especially wearying about that journey?" the King asked, puzzled. "It wasn't too far."

"It was Asmodeus' strange behavior that puzzled and worried me," Benaiah said, seating himself. "Listen, O King. In one village he brushed against a palm tree and uprooted it."

"Uprooted a tree?" Solomon repeated.

Benaiah nodded. "Just by brushing against it. I asked him why, of course, but he said he wouldn't tell me his secrets. Then he very kindly set a blind man on the right path when he had strayed from it, and with great gentleness he led a drunkard to the park where he could lie and sleep on some soft grass."

"Well, that was nice of him," said King Solomon.

"Wait, Your Majesty, I'm not through," Benaiah said. "In the next village we passed a wedding party. Everyone was joyous and they laughed and sang songs. And what do you think Asmodeus did? He burst into tears!"

"Weeping?" asked the King. "At a wedding? Why?"

Benaiah shook his head gloomily. "He wouldn't tell me. Then a little further on, at a shoemaker's shop, we heard a man ask the shoemaker to make a pair of shoes for him that would last seven years. Well now, that's a very economical thing to do, and I for one saw nothing humorous about it. But Asmodeus? He burst out laughing. As if that weren't bad enough, we came upon a magician doing some very clever tricks and I, for one, enjoyed watching him very much. But Asmodeus? Oh no, he had to ridicule the man and laugh at him."

"Strange, strange," the King murmured, pulling at his ear. "I am good at riddles. I shall think about them and figure them out myself."

He went to his Throne Room where he could be all alone. And he thought. Why would the King of the Demons uproot a tree? Why would Asmodeus weep at a wedding party and laugh at a magician and a man who ordered a pair of shoes to last seven years? The King thought and thought until it was time for the noon-day meal. Then he thought and thought until it was time for the evening meal. Then he thought and thought until it was time to go to bed, and still he had not found the answers to the riddle of Asmodeus' strange behavior.

Well, thought the King, I cannot go to bed with these puzzles unsolved. He called the Prison Warden and told him to bring Asmodeus before him.

The Warden did as commanded and brought the King of the Demons to the King of Israel.

"Greetings, O Solomon," Asmodeus said.

"Greetings, Asmodeus," King Solomon answered. "I have an extremely important question to ask of you. But that I shall let wait until tomorrow. I know you have had a long journey and you are tired. And besides, I want your brains good and clear for that important question which I shall ask you tomorrow."

"Very well," Asmodeus said, turning to go.

"Wait," the King commanded. "Benaiah has told me of your strange behavior on your journey here. He told me that you uprooted a palm tree . . ."

Asmodeus interrupted. "And laughed at a magician and at a man who ordered a pair of shoes to last seven years and wept at a wedding party." He nodded. "Yes, I did all those things."

The King nodded too. "Now I am very good at riddles, but, I have been puzzling my brains all day, and I cannot find the explanation for your strange behavior."

"Oh, I shall be glad to tell you," Asmodeus said. "I would not tell Benaiah because he captured me. But the great King Solomon I shall tell, just because he is so good at puzzles and cannot figure out the reason for my behavior."

He chuckled.

The King said crossly, "Speak."

"Your Majesty," said Asmodeus. "I judge people according to their real character and not by the things they happen to do. I wept when I saw the wedding party because I knew the groom would die within a month."

"Oh, I see," King Solomon said. "And why did you laugh at the man who ordered the shoes?"

"I laughed at him who ordered shoes for seven years because he would not own them for seven days. I set the blind man on the right path because I knew he was a good and honest person."

"But why did you laugh at the magician?" the King asked.

Asmodeus began to laugh now. He laughed and laughed, and then he said,

"Oh, that was funny. Your Majesty, it was truly very funny. I laughed at the magician because he pretended to know so many magical things . . . but . . . he did not know that under his very feet lay a buried treasure!"

Laughing in his glee, Asmodeus went back to prison.

The Moor-Hen's Secret

The remarkable Shamir had been made at twilight on the sixth day of Creation. It was very small, no bigger than a barley corn. What made it remarkable was its power of cutting through the hardest stone, whether it was marble, granite or the hardest rock.

Now when Solomon was King of Israel, he needed the Shamir. He didn't need the Shamir for building his palace or his treasure house or the Hippodrome. But he needed it for the Temple. For the palace and the treasure house and the Hippodrome he could use iron tools to cut the stones from the quarries. But for the Temple he was not permitted to use iron tools because swords were made of iron and the Temple was the place where people would learn to pursue peace.

Therefore he had to have the Shamir. No one knew where the Shamir was hidden, except Asmodeus, the King of the Demons. That is why Solomon had sent his Lieutenant, Benaiah, to capture Asmodeus and bring him to the palace prison.

Now Asmodeus was the prisoner of King Solomon, waiting in the dungeon until Solomon would send for him and tell him why he had been captured.

Three days after Asmodeus had been brought from his mountain top in chains, the Warden appeared before King Solomon and begged him to release Asmodeus from his care. Asmodeus was a trouble-maker. He was mischievous. He refused to eat, and he was constantly making strange noises.

"Bring him here to me," the King commanded.

A few minutes later, Asmodeus, arrogant and scornful, stood before the King.

"You are reported to be causing great mischief," Solomon said sternly.

"Why not?" Asmodeus said saucily. "I am the King of the Demons. You cannot expect me to behave myself like a human prisoner, meek and without spirit. Besides, why do you keep me locked up? Why have you brought me here, O Solomon?"

"I need your help," King Solomon answered.

Asmodeus bowed, and smiled, mockingly. "You need *my* help? You, the great Solomon? Indeed, indeed!"

"Show a little more respect," King Solomon growled.

"Oh, Your Majesty." Asmodeus bowed low, but his smile was still mocking.

"I am building a great Temple," the King said. "I cannot get the stones quarried because I am prohibited from using any iron instruments. I have heard of the worm called the Shamir which splits stones wide open."

"Ah, the Shamir," Asmodeus said, and nodded. "Yes, the Shamir can split the hardest of stone."

King Solomon said, "They tell me that you know where the Shamir is to be found."

"Who told you?" Asmodeus shrieked, jumping up and down in fury. "Who are 'they'?"

King Solomon smiled at the excited king of demons. "What difference does it make who 'they' are? It is enough that I know that you know. Come, come, tell me where the Shamir is."

"I don't know," Asmodeus muttered, sitting down on the floor and sulking.

"Get up on your feet like a man," King Solomon said. "Tell me where to find the Shamir."

58

"Won't," mumbled Asmodeus.

"See here," the King said. "I don't mean to keep you imprisoned forever, you know. I brought you here only to help me find the Shamir. When you tell me that, and I find it, then I intend to release you."

"You do?" Asmodeus jumped to his feet. "Promise?"

"I promise," the King said.

"Very well, then. Listen." Asmodeus strode up and down in front of the throne, his chest thrown out, parading before the King. "When the Shamir was first created, on the sixth day of Creation, you know, at twilight, you know . . ."

He paused, looking mischievously at the King.

"Go on. Go on," Solomon said impatiently.

Asmodeus continued, "On the sixth day of Creation at twilight. God gave it to the Angel of the Sea to take care of. Now, of course, the Angel of the Sea was busy with so many other oceanic matters, he was afraid he would lose it. So he looked over all the animals carefully and decided that he could trust the Moor-Hen."

"The Moor-Hen?" King Solomon asked.

"The Moor-Hen," repeated Asmodeus. He leaned against the throne. "So the Angel of the Sea gave the Shamir into the safe-keeping of the Moor-Hen, and she makes good use of it. She flies about and finds mountains on which no one lives because they are nothing but rock. And with the Shamir she splits open these mountains and then the under-soil is revealed and becomes good for planting. Then people go and live in these mountains which have become fertile farmlands."

"Very good," King Solomon said, wondering why he had never known of this before.

"Yes indeed," Asmodeus said, perching familiarly on the arm of the throne.

"I must request that you get down off the throne and stand on the floor," Solomon said sternly.

"Oh?" Asmodeus jumped down to the floor. "You must forgive me, King Solomon. I am a king myself, you know, and whenever I see a throne, I think I should be sitting on it."

"At present you are my prisoner," the King said, not sure whether to laugh or be stern. "Continue about the Shamir."

"Yes, yes, the Shamir," Asmodeus said. "I can tell you what the Shamir is. I can tell you where the Moor-Hen has her nest. But I cannot tell you where the Shamir is. The Moor-Hen keeps it carefully hidden away and I think, yes really I think there is no one in the world who knows where that secret hiding place is."

"I shall find it," King Solomon said. "Just tell me where the Moor-Hen's nest is."

Asmodeus jumped up the last step before the throne and whispered in King Solomon's ear. When the King had heard everything Asmodeus could tell him, he sent him back to the prison.

Now the King was confronted with a most difficult task. He decided to entrust it to Benaiah to whom he always gave the important missions. He summoned him, told him where the Moor-Hen had her nest, and commanded him to go and find the Shamir.

This time Benaiah despaired of fulfilling the King's orders. When he was sent to capture Asmodeus, the King had given him a chain, a bundle of wool, a flask of wine and the magic ring. This time he gave him only a square piece of glass.

But Benaiah, relying on King Solomon's wisdom, did not complain. He kept his worries to himself, and set out on his journey immediately. He travelled for three days until he reached the foothills of the high mountain on the top of which the Moor-Hen lived. It took him one whole day to climb the mountain. There, at the very top, he found the big locust tree where the Moor-Hen had her nest.

Benaiah hid behind a huge rock for a long time to be sure that the Moor-

Hen was not at home. He heard her little chicks chirping in the nest, but not a sign of the mother-bird did he see. Finally he crawled out from behind the huge rock and climbed up into the tree. When he reached the nest he took the square piece of glass which King Solomon had given him out of his pouch and placed it over the top of the nest. Then he climbed down from the tree, and hid himself again behind the huge rock, and waited.

Along toward sunset the Moor-Hen came flying home. She flew right to the nest where her young chicks were waiting. But, when she got there, she found the nest covered with a large square of glass. She had some nice worms in her mouth which she dropped towards the waiting mouths of her chicks. But strange to tell, the worms stayed halfway towards the nest and did not reach the chicks.

"What strange thing is this," she thought. "Is it a stone? I can see through it."

She had never seen glass before and didn't know what it was. She tapped her beak against it. Then she tried to grab it off with her claws. She tried to shove it over with her beak. But she couldn't move it. She struggled with it for a while and then realized that she could not reach her chicks until she found a way through this strange wall of clear stone which had come so magically to cover her nest. There was only one way of removing this odd roof. That was to split it, and only the Shamir could shatter it.

So away she flew to her secret hiding-place. There in a lead basket filled with barley bran, she kept the Shamir hidden. In the lead basket was a woolen cloth. And in the woolen cloth was the Shamir.

The Moor-Hen held the woolen cloth firmly in her beak and flew back to her nest. She lighted on the square of glass which Benaiah had placed over the nest, removed the woolen cloth and in one second the Shamir shattered the glass. As it splintered, the Moor-Hen heard her chicks joyfully biting their food, and happily she started to wrap up the Shamir again in the woolen cloth. When it was safely wrapped up, the Moor-Hen spread her wings, ready to fly back to hide the Shamir in its secret hiding-place. Just as she fluttered her right wing, Benaiah, who had been watching from behind the big rock, threw back his head and gave forth a big and a terrible shout.

The Moor-Hen was so frightened by the shout, she dropped the Shamir! Benaiah pounced on it, picked it up and began to run down the mountainside before the Moor-Hen even realized what had happened.

Benaiah went quickly away from the mountain, hurried back to the palace to King Solomon and gave him the Shamir. King Solomon immediately ordered a piece of marble to be brought into the Throne Room. When it was set before him, he drew a line across the face of the marble with his fingertip and placed the Shamir on the beginning of the line. The Shamir crawled over the marble, and the stone split, sharp and clean, all down its length.

"Truly wonderful," King Solomon said. "Truly marvelous. It is strange that I never heard of this Shamir before. But then, I never had to build a Temple before."

He gave the demon Rabdos the Shamir to cut out the stones from the quarry. But since Rabdos was a demon, and King Solomon did not trust demons, he put a special guard of ten soldiers over Rabdos to see that he did not try to escape with the rare and miraculous worm.

Now that he had the Shamir, King Solomon was able to quarry out all the stone he needed with which to build the Temple in Jerusalem.

The Bottle That Walked And Talked

On a fine spring day, Solomon was hard at work, writing his *Book of Proverbs*. He had already finished writing his poem, *The Song of Songs,* and some day he hoped to write a book to be called *Kohelet.* He was full of thoughts and wanted to get them down on parchment, and he did not welcome any interruptions.

Benaiah came into the Library where the King was writing, but one glance showed him that the King was not to be disturbed. Benaiah went out, but turned back again, entered the Library and stood hesitating on the threshhold. He didn't know what to do. Finally he summoned his courage and spoke from the doorway.

"Your Majesty . . ."

"I am not to be disturbed," Solomon said without looking up.

Benaiah took two steps forward into the room. "But, Your Majesty . . ."

"I am not to be interrupted," Solomon muttered, still without looking up.

Benaiah took four more steps into the room. "But, Your Majesty, it is a matter of vital importance."

Solomon pushed aside the parchment impatiently, and stood up.

"Benaiah, you know that when I am writing, I do not wish to be disturbed."

"But, Your Majesty, there is a messenger here from Adares . . ."

"The King of Arabia?" Solomon frowned. "What message does he bring?"

"He is instructed to tell no one but you, O Solomon."

"Very well," Solomon said. "I must not turn away a messenger from the King of Arabia."

He strode out of the Library and into the audience chamber. There the messenger was waiting. He bowed low when he saw the King, and came forward and handed him a long parchment scroll.

Solomon took the scroll, opened it, and read: —

"O Solomon, my great and kind friend. Come and deliver me, I beg you, from an evil spirit which does great mischief in my land. My servants have tried to capture this mischievous spirit, but to no avail. This evil demon appears in the form of wind, and we are helpless. Deliver me, my friend, I beseech thee, from this trouble."

Solomon called in the Royal Scribe and to him he dictated an answer to the King of Arabia, saying that he would help rid his land of this mischievous spirit. This message was given to Adares' messenger who set out at once for Arabia.

Solomon, meanwhile, secluded himself in his inner chamber. There he opened the four windows, to the east, the west, the south and the north. Then at each of the windows he sent out his message to the Winds to come before him.

In a few moments there was a great rush of air and from the east window came the East Wind, and from the west window came the West Wind, and the North and South Winds blew in last.

They were almost out of breath, they had come so quickly.

"We are at your service, O Solomon," said the East Wind, who had had the shortest distance to come.

"My friend, the King of Arabia, is in trouble," the King said. "One of your friends has been making mischief."

He told them of the message he had received from Adares.

"That spirit is disguised as the wind?" the West Wind said. "Then there is nothing we can do to help you, O King. It is not truly one of our winds which is causing this trouble, but a demon who only disguises himself as the wind. Indeed, I do not know how we can help you."

The other Winds all nodded their heads which made quite a stir of air in the room.

"If it were one of our helpers," the South Wind said, "if it were a breeze or a gush of air or even a tornado, then we could help, O Solomon."

"But not if it is a spirit *disguised* as the wind," the North Wind said. "It always annoys me very much to have someone masquerade as one of us, but there is no help for it."

64

"Since you cannot help," Solomon said, "then blow on your way, O Winds, and I thank you for coming."

Each of the Winds departed, out through his own window.

The King sat and thought and finally decided what to do.

He called one of his messengers to him, gave him a leather bottle and his magic ring. Then carefully he gave him his instructions.

The messenger left for the land of Arabia, arriving there many days later.

First he requested an audience with the King, to tell him that Solomon had thought of a way of ridding the land of Arabia from the troublesome sprite. Then he concealed himself in a corner of the right courtyard, waiting for the spirit which disguised itself as the wind to appear. After a little while he realized that concealment was a mistake. He came out of the corner and walked boldly to the center of the courtyard and spoke aloud.

"See what a beautiful bottle I hold in my hands. Indeed, it is made of leather. Only something precious has the right to be in it. I wonder what I should put into it. Shall it be wine? Or rare perfume?"

At that moment there was a rush of wind around his legs, and then, right into the leather bottle, went flying the spirit disguised as the wind! Quick as a flash, the messenger corked the bottle, and thus he had the spirit captured.

He returned to the palace and was brought before the Arabian King.

He bowed. "Your Majesty, I have captured the evil spirit which has been plaguing you." He held up the leather bottle. "Here it is, imprisoned in this leather casing."

"Good!" exclaimed the King. "Oh good, very good. I am very grateful to you. And I am exceedingly grateful to King Solomon who sent such a wise messenger."

He gave the messenger a fine reward and a special gift of a beautiful white Arabian horse to take to King Solomon.

The messenger rode the white horse back to Jerusalem, holding the bottle tightly all the way. Finally he trotted into the palace courtyard. He dismounted and entered the palace to present himself and the bottle to the King. But just as he reached the audience chamber, the spirit imprisoned inside the bottle kicked and squirmed so violently that, try as he would, the messenger could not hold the bottle. It tumbled out of his hands and into the audience chamber it rolled.

King Solomon was sitting on his throne, interviewing several people, when suddenly he raised his eyes. There on the floor, he saw a bottle waddling towards him!

"Now, O Spirit, let us see if you can bring up that stone."

"Whoever heard of a bottle walking!" the King exclaimed. "Who and what are you, O Bottle?"

The Bottle waddled to the throne, and bowed low.

"O Solomon, O King, I am the wind which your servant captured in Arabia."

"Ah fine," the King said. "Now you are imprisoned and can no longer work mischief in the land of Arabia."

"But I am very unhappy, Your Majesty," the Bottle said. "What wind likes to be bottled up? Oh please, Your Majesty, please release me, and I promise never to be mischievous again."

"Now, now, I don't believe your promise means very much," King Solomon said.

"It does, it does," the Bottle insisted, bobbing up and down. "I mean every word of it, I do. Let me prove it. Test my sincerity. Give me some task to perform. I shall gladly do anything you ask of me, and then you will know that I mean from now on only to be helpful, and never again mischievous."

"Very well," said the King. "I have a difficult problem which no one has been able to solve, not one of my servants, not even the cleverest. If you can accomplish this task, then I shall set you free to be a good and a helpful servant hereafter."

"Command me!" the Bottle cried.

"In the Red Sea," King Solomon said, "is a gigantic stone which I would like to use as a cornerstone for the Temple. No one has been able to get it out of the sea for me. Can you?"

"Yes, yes," the Spirit in the Bottle said. "Just let me out of this bottle and send me in a huge ship . . ."

"I shall send you in a huge ship," the King promised. "And let you out of the bottle when we reach the sea."

Two days later the expedition was ready to go. King Solomon himself went, with Benaiah, and many servants. They sailed on and on until they reached the Red Sea.

"This is the spot where that gigantic stone is to be found," the Captain of the ship said.

Solomon, holding the leather bottle in which the spirit was captured, followed by his entourage, went up on the deck of the ship. Then he said,

"I can do it!" the Spirit cried from inside the leather bottle. "I can do it. Just let me free."

"A word of warning, O Spirit," Solomon said. "If you break your promise or fail to bring up that stone, I shall consign you forever to the bottom of the sea."

"Let me out!" shouted the Spirit. "Only let me out."

"I release you," the King said. "But you are still in my power."

Solomon held the bottle firmly, and Benaiah pulled the cork out of it. A gush of wind came whistling out. It disturbed the air all around Solomon and his court. It whistled and blew, and moaned soft moans of relief at being free again. Then the moaning stopped and now the whistling of the wind sounded like a chuckle. Then came a voice saying,

"Free! Free! I am free again. Oh, I thank you, gracious King. I thank you, I do, I do indeed. And now I shall keep my promise."

The whistling faded away and the air grew still and more quiet as the wind blew away from the top of the boat. Down to the sea it blew, and soon the watchers on deck saw the waves rushing higher and higher to get out of the way. And then, right before their eyes there appeared a gigantic stone, pushed along by unseen fingers, right onto the ship, down into the very hold.

Then out of the wind came a voice saying, "Here, O Solomon, I have obeyed you. Now, O Solomon, will you release me?"

"Yes," the King said. "I release you now. Do no more mischief. Go and do only good deeds."

"Wheeeeee! I'll do only good!"

Away blew the wind and the air grew still once more.

The Tapestry of Stars

At last the great Temple was completed. When Solomon had begun this tremendous task, everyone wanted to have a part in it, and everyone did, even the small boys and girls, even the learned priests. Even the Pharaoh of Egypt did his part. He sent workmen to help Solomon, and so did Hiram, King of Tyre, who also sent thousands of logs of beautiful, clear cedar wood from the forests of Lebanon. Through the power of his magic ring, King Solomon forced all the demons to do the heavy labor. Asmodeus, the King of the Demons, told Solomon how to find the Shamir which split all the stones needed for the Temple. Hiram, the artist, labored hard and long for seven years.

And finally, it was finished.

Then King Solomon planted trees in the gardens surrounding the Temple. They were not, however, trees of wood. They were golden trees which magically bloomed and blossomed and gave forth golden fruit.

As soon as the Temple was completed, everyone expected that the King would dedicate it on the very next day. So when Solomon summoned them to appear in the courtyard of the Palace, they thought he would tell them what robes to wear for the dedication services, how the procession would form and where it would march. Instead, he said,

"Hear me, ye people. The mighty King of Egypt, Psusennes, my friend, the Pharaoh, has bestowed a great honor on me. He has given me his daughter as my wife."

Some of the people broke into cheers. Others were puzzled. Why did the great King Solomon want to marry an Egyptian Princess? But the King was speaking again, and everyone gave him close attention.

"On the morrow," declared the King, "at the fourth hour after the rise of the sun, I shall marry the Egyptian Princess. Today we shall celebrate. Go now, array yourselves, and be present within the hour at the Hippodrome for the games and the races."

Again some of the people cheered. But one man called out,

"What of the dedication of the Temple, O King?"

"On the day following my marriage to the Egyptian Princess," announced the King, "at the third hour after the rising of the sun, then shall we dedicate the Temple. Now go. Deck yourselves in your finery. Enjoy the races at the Hippodrome."

Everyone went home to dress for the gathering at the sports arena. Every group wore different colors for these games at the Hippodrome. The King and all his court dressed in light-blue garments. All the rest of the people of Jerusalem wore white. Travellers coming from all over the kingdom were told to wear red. And the foreign ambassadors and kings and noblemen who came with their gifts to the King, they wore green.

As the people began streaming towards the Hippodrome, they stopped at the entrance, at the two grilles which were ornamented with all sorts of animals. At each pillar were two golden lions and out of the jaws of the lions poured perfumes and spices which the people caught in their hands and sprinkled on their garments. Then they went into the arena and took their seats.

The royal pages came marching up the aisle, dressed in their light-blue satin suits, carrying their trumpets from which light-blue ribbons fluttered in the breeze. They blew their trumpets to announce the arrival of the King. Then came King Solomon himself, wearing his light-blue robes, leading by the hand the Egyptian Princess who would the next day become his bride. She was dressed in a light-blue flowing gown. King Solomon and the Princess were followed by all the court.

As soon as the royal party was seated, the races began. When the races and the games were over, the King provided banquets for all. Every banqueting table was served with rare wines and tastefully spiced foods. It was a day of gaiety and celebration.

On the morning of the wedding, the Egyptian Princess was sitting in her bedroom with her chief lady-in-waiting. Everything was in readiness for the wedding. The gown lay spread on the bed. The jewelled crown stood on a cedar chest. The lady-in-waiting put the white-satin sandals next to the crown, turned to the princess and said,

"Everything is ready for the wedding, O Princess. But the bride sits and frowns. Is anything wrong, Your Highness?"

The Princess made an impatient movement. "Didn't you hear the proclamation my lord Solomon made to the people?"

"Yes," the lady-in-waiting said, puzzled. "They have built a new Temple and tomorrow they will dedicate it to their God."

"No, no, you don't understand," the Princess said impatiently. "They do not have gods, these people. They have One God, an Unseen God whom they worship and I do not like it. They will not worship our Egyptian gods — all our lovely gods, our crocodile gods and our cat gods. Oh, who will worship the Goddess Isis with me? Oh, these people scorn to worship our gods. But they *must*. I shall make them."

"But my Princess," said the Lady-in-waiting. "How can you force them to worship Isis?"

The Princess smiled. She said softly, "I have a plan in mind. Come close . . ."

She whispered into the ear of the lady-in-waiting, giving her certain instructions.

Two hours later the Egyptian Princess and King Solomon were married, and since it was the wedding of a king, everything was as beautiful as it could be. The flowers which adorned the Throne Room where the wedding took place, and the banqueting hall, were the most perfect flowers ever seen in the land. The banquet tables were laden with the most luscious fruits, the rarest spices, and with every variety of food which had ever been eaten. Just before the wedding banquet started, a gorgeous bird from Barbary flew in through

70

the open window and settled down on the banquet table, right in front of the King and the new Queen. It was so magnificent a wedding that people spoke of it for many a year.

When the wedding was over, the King and the new Queen went to their own apartment in the palace and the King noticed that beautiful flower screens lined the walls of the room. But he failed to notice that the Queen had hung a tapestry across the ceiling, and that in this tapestry stars winked and twinkled, just as the real stars do.

"What beautiful flower screens," the King said.

At that moment, the sound of soft, lovely music came from behind the screens.

"And what beautiful music!" exclaimed the King.

The Queen smiled and said, "This music is played on the instruments which I brought from my own home, so that I would not be lonesome."

"A good idea," King Solomon said, not realizing that as each instrument was played, the Egyptian god whose instrument it was, was being prayed to at the same time.

The little ladies-in-waiting who sat cross-legged behind the flower-screens, playing the instruments all night, prayed to the Egyptian cat-god and the crocodile-god and the beetle-god and every god which the Egyptians worshipped. All night long the music played, and Solomon the King could not catch a wink of sleep.

Finally he said to the new Queen, "The music is keeping me awake, and I must get some sleep for I must be up very early in the morning to dedicate the new Temple."

"Why don't you let the priests dedicate it?" the Queen asked.

"That I cannot do," Solomon said. "The keys to the Temple are here under my pillow, and only I can dedicate the new Temple. So it is important for me to waken early. Therefore, let us have less music, please."

The Queen gave a sign and most of the music stopped. Just a low strumming from some zithers and harps continued. The ladies-in-waiting extinguished all the tapers and the room was in darkness.

The King fell asleep.

He woke up two hours after sunrise and started to get up.

"Why do you rise in the middle of the night?" the Queen asked.

"The middle of the night?" Solomon repeated. "Why it must be dawn. I must get up . . ."

"No, no, it is not dawn," said the Queen. "Look. The stars still shine."

She pointed overhead to the tapestry of the stars and King Solomon, with sleepy eyes, saw the artificial stars and thought that they were real, that it was indeed still night.

The King fell asleep.

He awoke about three hours after the rise of the sun and started to get out of bed.

"Why do you rise in the middle of the night?" the Queen asked again.

"Can it still be nighttime?" King Solomon asked. "It seems to me it must be early morning."

"No, no," the Queen said. "You see, the stars are still shining."

Solomon looked overhead at the tapestry of the stars and said,

"You are right, the stars are still shining."

And the King fell asleep again.

He awoke about four hours after the rise of the sun and started to get up.

"Why do you rise at dawn?" the Queen asked.

"Can it only be dawn?" the King asked. "It seems to me it must be mid-morning."

"No, no," the Queen said. "The stars still shine in the heavens."

Solomon looked overhead. All the stars in the tapestry twinkled brightly. And he said,

"Yes, the stars still shine. It must still be night."

But he did not fall asleep again.

Outside all the people had assembled at the third hour after the rise of the sun for the dedication of the Temple. And now by the fourth hour, they were getting impatient, and they began to mutter and to murmur, wondering if the Egyptian princess had bewitched King Solomon so that he could not rise to come and dedicate the Temple.

The chief councillors of the court approached Bathsheba, King Solomon's mother. Benaiah spoke for them.

"Do you know the reason for the King's delay, O Bathsheba?"

"Indeed, Benaiah, I do not," Bathsheba said. "Perhaps my son Solomon is ill."

"Perhaps we misunderstood the King," Benaiah said. "Perhaps today is not the day of the dedication."

"Today *is* the day," Bathsheba said firmly. "I shall go and talk to my son."

She went quickly through the palace until she came to the King's apartment. She called out,

"Solomon, Solomon, my son!"

"Yes, my mother," King Solomon answered. "I hear you. Why do you disturb me in the middle of the night?"

"It is not the middle of the night, my son," Bathsheba answered. "It is the fourth hour after the rising of the sun. The people await you. Come, dedicate the Temple."

"But that cannot be, my mother," Solomon called through the door. "The stars are still shining."

"The stars shine only in your bedroom, then, Solomon, my son," Bathsheba said sternly. "Outdoors, the sun gleams brightly."

"I shall come at once," Solomon called, jumping out of bed.

He looked overhead at the winking, twinkling stars. Then he turned and strode to the window, pulled aside the heavy curtains which shut out the light, and in through the window streamed the sun. Solomon looked up at the ceiling and the stars and saw them fade as the sunlight struck them. Then he knew he had been misled by a tapestry of stars.

"My Queen," he said. "Your tapestry of stars could bewitch me only for a little while, but now I see the light. I know the morning has come. The morning has come when we shall dedicate the Temple of the Lord. Your tapestry of stars could never truly hold back the sun nor stop the worship of the One True God."

The Bird, The King And The Throne

One day King Solomon was walking in his garden. The grass was green and the flowers bloomed and overhead the birds were flying, singing their songs. High up in the branches of one tree were two birds who were not singing. They were twittering; but those twitterings were more than just little sounds to King Solomon. They were words and sentences which he understood. He listened closely and he heard one bird say to the other:

"Ah, my lady love, there is nothing in the world I would not do for you."

"Nothing?" twittered the lady bird.

"Nothing," the male Bird said stoutly. "Even if you asked me to go to the palace and topple over the great throne of King Solomon, why even that I would do!"

At the foot of the tree, King Solomon heard that boast, and it made him angry. He strode back to the palace and with every step his rage mounted.

"That impudent bird," he said to himself. "That boastful, impudent bird, thinking he can topple over *my* throne. I cannot let such impudence go unpunished. Oh no, that bird must answer to me."

He walked to the eastern window and began a low twittering sound. It was his special call to the birds who lived in the east which they understood as a command from the King to come into his presence. As soon as they heard it, they came winging their way from the east. Then the King went to the west window where he whistled his twittering command, and the birds from the west came flying to the palace. King Solomon walked to the north window and to the south and at both those windows he sent forth his bird call, and the birds from the north and the south answered his summons too.

74

And so, of course, amongst all the birds in the kingdom who came flying at the King's command was the little bird from the King's garden, who had made his boast to his lady love that he could topple over the King's throne.

Now this bird was just a plain brown bird, not more colorful nor any bigger than a sparrow. He landed on the east windowsill next to a beautiful yellow finch.

"Why do you suppose the King called us together?" the Brown Bird asked.

"I don't know," the Finch answered. "But all the birds have come."

The Brown Bird looked around and saw every bird, those with red breasts, and those with orange tails tipped with black. The Bird of Paradise was there, and the Oriole, the Bluebird and the Mockingbird. One of each kind of bird from all over the kingdom stood perched on the windowsills of the palace. At first there was a great twittering and chittering and twerping that filled the large Throne Room. Then slowly the chirpings grew fainter and fainter until all the birds were still. The King was ready to speak.

"My fine-feathered friends," he said. "I thank you for coming at my bidding."

"Indeed, Your Majesty," said the Mockingbird. "We could do nothing else when the King himself has summoned us."

"Indeed, indeed," echoed the Parrot.

King Solomon nodded his head. "For some time now my throne has been completed. And today I realized that my friends, the birds, had never seen this unusual throne."

"Ah, but we have heard of it," the little Brown Bird spoke up eagerly.

King Solomon looked right at the little bird and thought, yes, he is impudent; you see, with all these other birds here, he speaks right up.

"We have heard of it," the little Brown Bird repeated. "And I have tried to peek in, I admit." The little Brown Bird gave a soft bird-laugh. "But the heavy hangings at the windows of the palace were always drawn together."

Again King Solomon nodded. "But today you shall all see the throne."

The Parrot screeched in excitement, and the Owl hooted, and the Crow crowed with delight. But no one was more excited than the little Brown Bird. He flew away from the windowsill right to King Solomon's shoulder, then back to the windowsill, then back to the King. He was so excited he couldn't stand still.

"Come," said the King to the little Brown Bird. "Since you are too excited to remain still, come here. You may perch on my shoulder and remain with me while I show the magnificent throne."

"Me?" The little Brown Bird almost choked with excitement. "Me, me, I, I, you mean I may rest on the shoulder of the King?"

Not waiting for an answer, not giving the King a chance to change his mind, the little Brown Bird flew straightaway to the royal shoulder and settled himself gently, but firmly on the ermine and purple velvet.

The King turned to walk towards the throne. All the birds began their soft winging behind him, flying gently, as the King led the way. He stopped and pulled a curtain aside and there was revealed the throne. The birds all trilled their surprise.

The Bird of Paradise ruffled her feathers, not sure that *she* should admire the throne. But all the other birds oh'd and ah'd in their own particular ways, but none oh'd and ah'd louder and longer than the little Brown Bird, so amazed at the sight of the throne that he could hardly stand still on the King's shoulder.

No other throne like this existed in the whole world. From Ophir had come the fine gold which covered it. It was made of marble, and covered with every imaginable jewel in the world, diamonds and pearls and rubies. And, leading up to the throne, were two pairs of six steps.

King Solomon walked to the first pair of steps. There on each of the six steps were two golden lions and two golden eagles. The golden eagles looked fierce and the golden lions looked menacing. All the birds fell back a wing-length or two as they saw that King Solomon was going to mount the steps. The little Brown Bird fluttered its wings as though to fly off the King's shoulder.

"Do not be afraid, little Brown Bird," the King said. "Just stay on my shoulder and I shall lead you past the lions."

The King walked up the first set of six steps. Then he faced the second set of six steps. On the first one, leading to the throne itself, crouched an ox and opposite him a lion. As the King put his foot on the first step, the ox lowed and the lion roared. And the little Brown Bird shivered and shook. But he found courage to pipe up,

"I think, Your Majesty, I had better go home. I just remembered some important business . . ."

King Solomon smiled. "What could be more important than seeing King Solomon's throne?"

The Lion and the Eagle from the first pair of steps came and led the King

76

to the second step leading to the throne. On the second step were a wolf and a lamb. As the King put his foot on the second step, the lamb bleated and the wolf howled. And the little Brown Bird shook and shivered, and squeaked,

"O dear King, I must go now. I'll come another day . . ."

"What better day could there be," the King said, smiling, "for seeing the throne of King Solomon?"

And the Lion and the Eagle of the second pair of steps came and led the King to the third step leading to the throne. On the third step stalked a leopard and a goat. As the King put his foot on the third step, the goat bleated and the leopard growled. And the little Brown Bird quivered and quaked, and screeched,

"Oh my, something tells me my nest is on fire. I have seen enough of the throne, Your Majesty. I'd better hurry away . . ."

King Solomon smiled again, and said, "But you haven't seen all of it, my little brown friend. Come, come, here are the Eagle and the Lion of the third step to lead us to the fourth step which leads to the throne itself."

On the fourth step stood an eagle and a peacock, and as the King put his foot on the step, the Peacock gobbled and the Eagle screeched. The little Brown Bird turned his quivering head and saw that by now the birds who had come into the throne room had all safely retreated to the window-sills where they perched, chattering and twittering away in their excitement, wondering what was going to happen to the little Brown Bird.

Indeed, he wondered too, as the Lion and the Eagle of the fourth step came and led the King to the fifth step of the stairs leading to the throne. There on the fifth step were a Falcon and a Rooster, and as the King put his foot on the fifth step, the Rooster crowed and the Falcon screeched. The little Brown Bird could hardly catch his breath until he saw that on the sixth step leading to the throne, the animals made of gold were a Hawk and a Sparrow.

The little Brown Bird took a long, shuddering sigh, knowing that the Hawk and the Sparrow were feather-friends and would never hurt him, even if they were made of gold. So he took another deep breath and looked at the throne itself over which hung a golden candlestick, with golden lamps, pomegranates, snuff dishes and chains and lilies.

King Solomon moved forward, sat himself on the throne and a great golden Eagle set the royal crown on his head. Then a golden Dove came flying and lighted on the King's other shoulder. The King nodded to the Dove, turned to the little Brown Bird, and said,

"Well, friend Bird. And how do you like my throne?"

"Like it!" stuttered the Bird. "Like it! It is the most magnificent, the most wonderful, the most . . . Well really, Your Majesty, really I am speechless. I have never seen anything like it. My friends and I fly all over the world, and there is nothing we have not seen, and when we come back, we compare notes, you know. And nowhere have I ever seen or heard of a throne like this."

"Yes," King Solomon said, and nodded his head. "I know it to be the most magnificent throne in the whole world. And you agree?"

"Yes, yes, I agree," the Bird said quickly. "I just told you, Your Majesty, that I know it to be the most magnificent, the most wonderful, well, as I said before, words just fail me!"

"Then," the King said softly, turning his big and wise eyes upon the fluttering Bird. "Then, my little brown friend, how did you dare tell your lady love that you were going to topple over King Solomon's throne?"

"Who, me?" said the Bird. "I? Oh, King Solomon, do you think I would say such a ridiculous thing."

The Bird fluttered his wings, wishing he were far, far away.

"Yes, I heard you say it, with my very own ears."

"Oh dear, caught in the act," murmured the little Brown Bird.

"Caught in the act," the King repeated, trying to look stern, but he did want to laugh.

"Oh, dear King," the Bird pleaded. "You know I didn't mean anything so foolish, don't you? You're such a wise King. You're the wisest man in the world, aren't you?"

"No flattery," King Solomon growled, trying to keep from laughing out loud.

"But you *are* the wisest man in the world," the Bird insisted. "And you know how it is, dear King, with us males. Wise or foolish, we do try to impress our lady loves with how big and strong we are, don't we?"

Then the King did laugh. "So that's what you were trying to do, eh? Impress your lady love?"

"Yes, yes," the Bird said eagerly, sighing to himself as he realized that Solomon understood him. What a narrow escape! "Yes, I wanted her to think I was stronger than any bird in the world."

"Very well, then," King Solomon said. "Go back to your lady friend. Tell her about this throne with its animals made of gold. And tell her that you can vanquish every animal on King Solomon's throne."

"Thank you, thank you," the Bird called, as he began to fly away.

"And tell her, too," King Solomon called after him. "Tell her that you can topple over King Solomon's throne. I won't mind it at all."

The little Brown Bird winged his way into the garden and up to the tallest limb of the tallest tree, where his lady bird was waiting.

"Where have you been, my love?" she cried.

"Toppling over King Solomon's throne," he chirped.

79

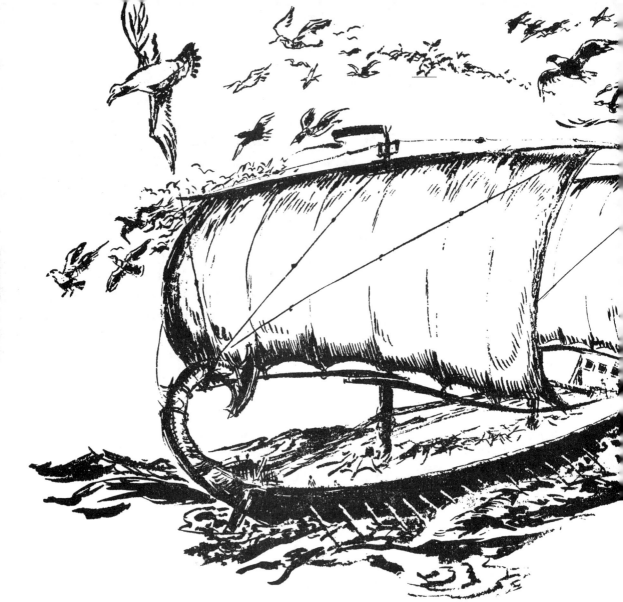

The Land of Sheba

In King Solomon's garden one day, a Bluebird and a Mockingbird were sitting on a low branch of a tree, just talking, when suddenly, the Hoopoe came flying towards them. He reached for the branch with his claws and almost missed, but grasped it in time, and clung to it, gasping for breath.

"Well, well," said the Mockingbird. "I haven't seen you for a long time. Where have you been?"

"Can't you see he's out of breath?" the Bluebird said. "Let him catch his wind before you ask him questions."

"No, no," the Hoopoe gasped. "I must see King Solomon immediately. But I had to stop to rest . . ."

"Well, you'll get a good, long rest," the Mockingbird said, laughing his mocking laugh, "because the King is away on a journey."

"Oh, no!" cried the Hoopoe. "Oh, I was so sure he'd be home. Tell me where he's gone and I'll fly after him."

"You can't do that," the Bluebird said. "Because no one knows where he's gone."

The Mockingbird chuckled. "When King Solomon goes sailing away on his magic carpet, indeed, who knows where he goes? He goes far, far away."

"Oh, he's gone on his magic carpet?" the Hoopoe asked, then sat shaking his head, knowing that he could never try to catch up with the King, even if he knew which way he'd gone. Only the Eagle was strong enough to keep up with the King's magic carpet.

The Hoopoe was greatly disappointed because he wanted to give his news to the King at once. But there was nothing to do except to wait for him to return from his latest adventure on the magic carpet. In the meantime the Hoopoe could rest, and he needed a rest, because he had come from a long, long journey.

Three days later, as all the birds in the garden were lazily singing their songs in the bright sunshine, they heard a sound they all recognized and loved. King Solomon was calling to them. He had returned from his journey and perhaps he would tell them about his latest adventures. They all began beating their wings, flying fast through the open windows of the palace, to get to the King's throne.

But fastest of all flew the Hoopoe. He speeded directly to the King's hand and perched on his forefinger.

"O King," the Hoopoe said. "I know you have a marvelous adventure to tell us about. But please, Your Majesty, I have just returned from a three-month's journey and I must tell you what I discovered."

"Indeed." The King seemed displeased. "I have just returned on my magic carpet from a glorious adventure . . ."

"But please," the Hoopoe said, interrupting the King.

All the birds gasped. They were shocked, even the Mockingbird. And the King gasped too, surprised to have one of the birds interrupt him. But when he saw how serious the Hoopoe was, the King realized that perhaps this was indeed something important.

So he nodded slowly, and said, "Speak, Hoopoe. Speak."

"These past three months," the Hoopoe said, "I have spent flying about the world to see if there were any country which was not subject to my lord, Solomon the King."

"All the countries serve our King," the Peacock said proudly.

"Yes," answered the Hoopoe. "All but one. Far in the east, in the land of Sheba, I have found a city called Kitor."

"Kitor?" said the King. "I have not heard that name."

The Hoopoe nodded and continued. "This land in the east is fabulously rich. The mud of the riverbanks is more valuable than silver. The dust of the street is more valuable than gold. The people of Kitor are peace-loving. They know neither how to shoot an arrow nor fling a spear. And their ruler . . ."

"Yes, yes," King Solomon prompted. "Their ruler?"

"Their ruler," the Hoopoe said slowly, "is a woman. She is called the Queen of Sheba. Now, O Solomon, with your permission I shall return to Kitor in the land of Sheba, and I shall order their queen to become a slave to my lord, Solomon the King."

The King said, "Good. You shall return to Sheba. I shall give you a letter to take to the Queen."

He turned to Benaiah standing at his side, and commanded,

"Summon the Royal Scribe."

When the Royal Scribe came, the King dictated a letter and, when the Scribe had finished writing it, he bound it to the foot of the Hoopoe.

"Now I shall go to the land of Sheba and claim it for my King," the Hoopoe said, testing his wings, preparing to fly.

But King Solomon had one more question. "And when you have done all this and shall return, how shall I reward the faithful Hoopoe?"

"O mighty King," the Hoopoe said. "The only reward I seek is to serve the King."

"Then go," said Solomon.

"Farewell," cried the Hoopoe.

As he spread his wings and swooped up into the sky, all the birds cried, "Let us go with you."

And away they went, flying after the Hoopoe, over mountains and trees and rivers and lakes. Long, long they flew until they reached the land of Sheba and the city of Kitor. They arrived just as the sun was setting.

The Queen of Sheba worshipped the Sun as her god. Now that the time of day had come when the Sun shed its last beams over the earth before retiring for the night and its darkness, the Queen came to say good night to her Sun-god. She came out into the garden, which was rich in fruit trees and fragrant with the perfume of many spices and flowers. She prepared to raise her arms in worship to the Sun, when, suddenly, the light of the Sun was blotted out. In great alarm, she raised her eyes to see why the light of her god was darkened and what manner of thing dared to interrupt her worship.

There, flying across the face of the Sun, were hundreds of birds. They were flying towards her, their wings beating rapidly. The Queen of Sheba stood very still until one of the birds separated itself from the others. It was the Hoopoe. He swooped down and came to rest on the branch of a rosebush near her face. He fluttered his wings and held out his leg to show that a message was tied to it. The Queen untied it and read it. Then, in great alarm, she sent her lady-in-waiting to summon the princes and nobles of her kingdom to come and meet with her in the great, open amphitheater bordered by the willow trees.

When they had all assembled, looking wonderingly at the huge flocks of birds fluttering their wings near the Queen, she rose, holding the letter in her hand, and silenced them all, the princes and the nobles and the birds, with one gesture of her hand. Then she spoke, her voice ringing out over the vast amphitheater.

"These birds have brought me a message from King Solomon."

"King Solomon? Who is this King called Solomon?" one prince asked haughtily, shrugging his shoulders. "I have never heard of him."

The Queen of Sheba answered him. "He writes that he is a powerful monarch, that God has appointed him king over the beasts of the field, the birds of the air, the demons, the spirits and all manner of things."

"But not king of men." One nobleman laughed.

"Ah yes," the Queen answered. "He says further that all the kings in the world come and pay homage to him. And he invites me, nay, he warns me, to come and pay him homage or else . . ."

"Or else?" her chief adviser asked scornfully.

"Or else," the Queen continued. "He will send out his legions against me."

One councillor yawned and said, "And who may these legions be?"

The Queen of Sheba read from King Solomon's letter:

"You ask, who are these kings, legions, and riders of King Solomon? The beasts of the field are my slaves, the birds my riders, the demons, spirits and shades of the night my legions. If you will come and pay homage to me, I shall give you great honor. If not, the beasts will slay you in the fields."

"It sounds like the ravings of a madman," said one of the princes. "I should pay no attention to it, O Queen, if I were you."

"Quite right," said another prince. "I have never heard of this Solomon, and his threats leave me quite unafraid."

But they did not leave the Queen unafraid. She paid no attention to the indifference and scorn of her noblemen, but decided to respond at once to the letter. She would send Solomon some valuable gifts.

She ordered ten vessels made ready and in them were loaded gifts of pearls and diamonds, rubies and balsam trees. Then she ordered the ladies-in-waiting to assemble three thousand girls, all born in the same year, in the same month, on the same day, and in the same hour. The ladies-in-waiting were to see that the three thousand girls were all the same height and the same weight.

"Then," said the Queen of Sheba. "Clothe them all in purple garments."

Then she ordered the princes to assemble three thousand young men, all born in the same year, in the same month, on the same day, and in the same hour. The princes were to see that the three thousand young men were all the same height and the same weight.

"Then," said the Queen of Sheba. "Clothe them all in purple garments."

The ladies-in-waiting and the princes rushed to do her bidding. When they had completed their tasks, the Queen commanded the three thousand young men and the three thousand young girls to board the ten vessels.

The ships set sail and on the shore, to speed them, were the Queen and the princes and noblemen of her realm. And clustered on the shore, too, were the Hoopoe and the hundreds of birds who had flown with him to the land of Sheba. When they saw the last sail of the last ship unfurled in the breeze, the Queen of Sheba tied a parchment scroll to the foot of the Hoopoe. It was her answer to King Solomon. Then the birds were ready to leave. With a loud shrilling from their many throats, with the Hoopoe leading the way, they began to fly back to the land of their King.

Back they flew, over lakes and rivers and mountains, until finally they reached King Solomon's palace. The King was assembled with his court waiting impatiently. Would the Hoopoe be successful in his errand? Or would he fail?

Suddenly, a bird-watcher came running in, crying,

"The birds! The birds return!"

In through the open windows hundreds of birds came flying. The Hoopoe darted right to the throne to the right arm-rest, gasping for breath. The King stroked his head, while the Royal Scribe, holding a very large book in front of him, called all the names of all the birds to see that everyone was present. By that time the Hoopoe had regained his breath, and the King had taken the letter off the Hoopoe's foot.

"What luck, O Hoopoe?" asked King Solomon. "What luck did you have with the Queen of Sheba?"

"I do not know, my lord," the Hoopoe answered. "Her reply is contained in this letter. But this I do know. The Queen has sent you ten ships laden with fine woods and precious stones, and six thousand youths garbed in purple cloth."

"It is a fine gift," the King said. "But it is not sufficient if she herself does not come."

He opened the letter from the Queen of Sheba and read:
"O King, O Solomon, seven years are required to journey from the city of Kitor in the land of Sheba to the city of Jerusalem in the land of Israel. But I, the Queen of Sheba, shall hasten. I shall present myself in the city of Jerusalem within three years."

"Success!" Benaiah exclaimed. "Success! The Queen of Sheba will come."

"Success," repeated King Solomon, and turned to the Hoopoe. "The success is due to this little bird, to the Hoopoe. And now I must reward you. Ask what you will and I shall grant it to you for bringing under my dominion a rich city and a great land."

"There is no gift I desire, O Solomon," the Hoopoe answered. "I did tell Your Majesty that it was reward enough for me if I serve my lord and master, Solomon the King."

"That is fine," Solomon said. "Your loyalty pleases me. But reward you I must. Come, isn't there one little thing you have always set your heart on? Isn't there one thing you have admired more than any other? What can I give you?"

The Hoopoe was silent for a moment, struggling with desire and timidity and the fear of being too bold. Then he sputtered,

'Just one thing, O King. The thing I have admired most in the world is the crown which Solomon the King wears on his head."

"What!" shouted Benaiah, thinking the Hoopoe wanted the King's crown. But Solomon laughed at him. "How ridiculous is your anger, Benaiah.

86

The crown of King Solomon would cover over the whole of the Hoopoe so that he could never see the light, nor flutter his wings again. No, no, Benaiah. The Hoopoe does not want *my* crown. He only wants a crown like mine. Very well," he said to the Hoopoe. "You shall have a crown."

He commanded the Royal Goldsmith to fashion a tiny crown made of gold, exactly to match the Royal Crown. It took the Royal Goldsmith only one day to fashion such a tiny crown, not larger, perhaps, than a green pea. And this King Solomon set upon the little head of the Hoopoe, and ever since then, as Solomon's reward, the Hoopoe has worn a crown-like crest over his small forehead.

The Queen's Riddles

For three years King Solomon waited for the Queen of Sheba to come to Jerusalem as she had promised. During that time he inquired amongst all the neighboring kings and those who ruled farther to the east about the Queen of Sheba and what they knew of her. One king, who lived closest to the city of Kitor in the land of Sheba, was able to tell King Solomon a great deal about her. One thing in particular King Solomon was glad to hear, that the Queen, besides being very, very rich, and very, very beautiful, and very, very charming, was extremely clever at riddles.

Now King Solomon loved riddles. He always guessed them, because he was so wise. And there was nothing he liked better than hearing a new riddle. His friend Hiram, the King of Tyre, was also good at riddles, and Hiram and Solomon used to spend many an hour telling puzzles to each other. Hiram didn't always guess Solomon's riddles. But Solomon always guessed Hiram's, and by now they had gotten a little stale and a little old, and Solomon was eager to hear some brand-new ones. So he waited impatiently for these three years to pass and the Queen to come with her puzzlers.

Meanwhile he went on with his preparations for her visit. Since she was sending him six thousand youths garbed in purple, he decided to match her gift exactly. He sent his councillors to find three thousand girls all born in the same year, in the same month, on the same day and at the same hour. They had to be of the same height and weight.

"Garb them," said the King, "in gowns of light blue."

Then he sent his princes to find three thousand young men, all born in the same year, in the same month, on the same day and at the same hour. They had to be of the same weight and the same height.

"Garb them," said the King, "in garments of light blue."

Next he commanded his Royal charioteers to assemble ten chariots and to pile high in them fine silks and woolens, clusters of diamonds and rubies and all kinds of precious stones. These he would present to the Queen of Sheba in exchange for the ten shiploads which she was sending him.

When that was done, he summoned the Royal Architects and the Royal Builders and commanded them to build a house made of glass. This he would present to the Queen to use as her palace during her stay in the land of Israel.

Finally all was ready, and the three years of waiting had passed. When the time for her arrival had come, the King sent Benaiah to meet her. Benaiah drove in the royal chariot to the sea coast and sent the proper salute to the Queen's flagship. The message of greeting was relayed to the Queen's ship, and, all in royal order, she disembarked. Benaiah made a fitting speech of welcome and, in the royal chariot conducted the Queen from the sea coast inland to Jerusalem to the palace made of glass. There waited King Solomon to greet her.

"Welcome, O Queen of Sheba. Welcome to the land of Israel."

The Queen bowed and said, "I thank you, Solomon, King of Israel, for your royal greetings."

Then, standing at the entrance of the palace made of glass, King Solomon and the Queen of Sheba watched as the six thousand youths clothed in purple, the gift of the Queen, and the six thousand youths clothed in light blue, the gift of the King, passed in review. Then the chariots piled high with silks and fine woolens and all manner of costly jewels, were brought to the palace of glass for the Queen.

That evening, at a sumptuous banquet, the King presented the Queen of Sheba to his court and all the neighboring kings whom he had invited. When the meal was finished, the Queen of Sheba turned to King Solomon and said,

"I have enquired of you from my friends, O King, and I have heard that you are a man of great wisdom."

The King bowed his head slightly. "And I have enquired of you, O Queen, and have heard that you know many riddles with which I should like to test my wisdom."

"Agreed," the Queen said, and smiled. "Shall we begin now?" And without waiting for his consent, she asked,

"The first riddle: Who is he who neither was born nor has died?"

Without hesitation, Solomon said, "The Lord of the world, blessed be He."

"Correct," cried the Queen of Sheba. "The second riddle: What land is that which has seen the sun but once?"

And the King answered, "The bed of the Red Sea on the day when it was divided; it saw the sun then, and the waters returned and covered it ever afterwards."

"Good." The Queen nodded her head. "The third riddle: There is something which when living moves not, yet when its head is cut off, it moves."

"It is the ship in the sea," the King said quickly. "When it is a living tree, it is rooted in the soil. When cut down and built into a ship, it moves across the waters."

At that moment the Royal Musicians interrupted to play and sing a few songs, and the Queen of Sheba used those few moments to whisper directions to her Chief Chamberlain. He nodded his head and left the room. When the music ended, the Chief Chamberlain returned and whispered to the Queen who nodded.

90

King Solomon turned to her and said, "I am ready to resume the riddles, if Your Majesty is ready."

"I am quite ready," she said, smiling. "The next riddle: Who were the three that ate and drank on earth, and yet were not born of parents?"

The King moved his hand impatiently. This was too easy. "Why, the three angels who visited Abraham, of course."

The Queen of Sheba felt King Solomon's impatience. She had not expected him to answer so easily. She had used up some of her best riddles. She thought hard to find one he might not know. Then she said,

"What was that which was not born, yet life was given to it?"

King Solomon fidgeted. He was bored. He had expected so much entertainment from the new riddles of a far-off land. And he was disappointed. He sat gloomily, brooding, until the Queen said,

"Can't you answer this riddle, Your Majesty?"

The King started. "I beg your pardon, O Queen. I was not listening."

She flushed with annoyance because she knew he was bored. But she repeated,

"What was that which was not born, yet life was given to it?"

And the King said in a voice of weariness and boredom, "The Golden Calf."

He gave a signal for the royal dancers to entertain. While the dancing was going on, the Queen of Sheba scarcely saw a single movement. She was so busy thinking. When the dancing was over, she said,

"I have another riddle, O King: Who was he that was born yet died not?"

King Solomon answered without hesitation, "Elijah."

"One more riddle for this evening," the Queen of Sheba said. "I shall save my best one for another time. But for today, this last one: What is this? It comes from the earth, it is poured out like water, yet it lights the house?"

Solomon laughed. "The answer to that is oil."

"Now," she said. "I have something to show you."

She clapped her hands and in through the north door came twenty people, all the same height and the same weight and all dressed alike, in green cloaks that fell to the floor covering their feet, with long sleeves covering their hands and with hoods covering their faces. They walked in front of the King and stood about ten feet away, all in one line.

Then the Queen of Sheba said, "Ten of these are girls and ten of these are young men. Tell me, O King, which are the girls and which are the young men?"

The King made a signal to one of the servants and asked for a bowl of sugared dates. When they were brought, he ordered the servant to pass them out to the twenty young people standing in front of them. Each one reached out to take the sugared dates, but ten of them took them in their bare hands while the other ten, before taking the sugared dates, reached into pockets of their robes, brought out white gloves which they put on their hands, and then took the dates.

King Solomon laughed, turned to the Queen of Sheba and said,

"The ten with the white gloves are girls. The ten with the bare hands are young men."

The Queen of Sheba laughed with him, dismissed the twenty young people, and then said,

"I confess myself vanquished by the wisdom of the King."

"It matters not, dear Queen," the King said graciously. "To hear your riddles was the smallest part of our interest in meeting the Queen of Sheba. Remain here, live in the palace of glass that I have built for you, and give our court the pleasure and the profit of your royal presence."

"I thank you, O Solomon," the Queen of Sheba said. "I shall remain for several moons, observing at the court of the wise King of Israel so that I may take back to my own country what wisdom I may learn here."

The King of Israel and the Queen of Sheba bowed to each other in friendship.

The Impudent Bee

King Solomon awoke one morning from what he thought was a bad dream. But the moment he sat up in bed and felt his nose, he shook his head gloomily. It had not been a bad dream. He called to his valet to bring him a mirror. He took one look in the mirror. He took a second look in the mirror and saw that his nose, his Royal Nose, was swollen and red like a big red apple!

"How did this happen?" he roared. "It hurts me!"

The valet backed away. "Your Majesty, it's the bite of an insect."

"An insect bite? What insect had the impudence to bite my Royal Nose?"

The valet crept to the door.

"Look how swollen and red my nose is," the King shouted. "My Royal Nose." And then he laughed. "It should be purple, if it's royal, eh?" But he stopped laughing and became angry again, as angry as his nose was red. "What bit me?" he demanded of the frightened valet.

"Indeed, sir, Your Majesty," the valet whimpered, creeping two steps closer to the bed. "Indeed, sir, it looks to me like the sting of a bee."

93

"The sting of a bee, eh?" The King studied his nose again in the mirror. "Ah yes, indeed, that's exactly what it looks like, a bee sting." He flung the mirror onto the pillow. "Now what shall I do?"

The valet, thinking he was talking to him, came another step towards the bed, and said, timidly, "They say, sir, Your Majesty, that vinegar is good for a bee sting."

"Vinegar!" shouted the King. "Vinegar, indeed. Run. Get the Royal Physician."

The valet ran to get the doctor, while the King sat glowering into the mirror, turning his face to the left, then to the right, looking at it from this angle, from that angle. No, nothing helped. No matter how he looked at his nose, it was only red and angry looking, and swollen to twice its normal size.

In a few moments the Royal Physician came running into the room.

"Your Majesty," he stammered. "What is the trouble? What hurts . . ."

And then he saw the red and swollen nose, and he almost burst out laughing. He caught himself in time, and coughed instead. He coughed and coughed until his face was as red as the King's nose.

"You are laughing at me," the King accused.

"Oh no, Your Majesty," gasped the Royal Physician. "No, no, something got caught in my throat. Now, let us see. What is wrong here?"

He examined the nose, this way and that, to the left, to the right, but there was nothing to do when he finished his examination but to shake his head and sigh.

"Well? Well?" demanded the King. "It's an insect bite, even my valet knows that. What insect bit me, sir?"

"Why, ah." The Royal Physician sputtered and coughed. "A bee stung you."

"Indeed!" The King glowered. "Even my valet knows that. And what do you propose doing for it, sir?"

"Well now." The Royal Physician rubbed his hands together and smiled hesitatingly. "A little vinegar . . ."

"Vinegar!" shouted the King. "No. Never. Away with you. Out! Out of my sight, sir!"

The Royal Physician picked up his little bag and fled.

The King turned to his valet. "Tell my court to convene without me," he said. "Tell them . . . tell them . . . tell them the King is indisposed."

94

The valet rushed away to tell the court that the King was indisposed, but already the gossip had spread through the palace. Some of the noblemen snickered about the King's swollen nose, and some shook their heads in wonder that any bee could be so impudent as to sting the nose of the King!

The King thought it was impudence too. Still in his night-dress, he strode to the window which was open just an inch, thrust it wide open and began making a funny, buzzing sound that to anyone else would have sounded just as if he were clearing his throat. But a little Bee, sucking the honey from a flower near the window, heard the funny, buzzing sound, and she understood what it was. It was a message in Bee-language to all the Bees, and it said:

"I, King Solomon, hereby summon the Queen Bee to my presence. I, King Solomon, hereby summon the Queen Bee to my presence."

The King turned aside and went to get dressed, while the little Bee flew away to the rose gardens to tell the Bees working there to take the message to the Queen Bee. The Rose-Bees flew to the lilac-gardens to tell the Lilac-Bees to take the message to the Queen Bee. The Lilac-Bees flew away to the hyacinth-gardens to take the message to the Queen. And so one flower-bee flew to the next flower-bee until finally the message was given to the Tulip-Bee who flew right to the Queen Bee.

"O Queen Bee," gasped the Tulip-Bee. "King Solomon commands your presence."

"Very well," the Queen Bee said. "And thank you for bringing the message."

As she flew from garden to garden, she thanked every Bee she passed for bringing her the message from the King, until finally she landed right on the windowsill of the King's bedroom. There she paused for a moment to catch her breath. Then she began buzzing:

"Bz bzz bzzzz, Bz Bzzz z. Bz bzz bzz bzzzz bzzzzzzz,"

which, of course, the King understood to mean:

"I am here, O King. I am at your service."

King Solomon walked to the window. "Thank you, O Queen, for coming so promptly."

"I came as soon as I heard, Your Majesty. How may I serve you?"

"Look at my Nose!" the King thundered, pointing to the red and swollen Royal Nose.

"Oh, your poor nose," the Queen said.

"Stung by one of your bees!" accused the King.

The Queen curtsied and said, "Oh, I am so sorry, King Solomon. And I am so embarrassed to think that one of my subjects could have been so thoughtless as to bite the nose of the great King Solomon. I apologize, Your Majesty."

"Apologies are not enough. Find that Bee," the King ordered. "And send him here to me, at once."

"Yes, Your Majesty. Immediately."

The Queen Bee whirled around, flying rapidly out of sight. She flew from one flower garden to another, asking every Bee she met if he knew who had stung the Royal Nose. No one knew, until she came to the orchid garden, and there she found a young Bee who confessed. The Orchid-Bee admitted that he had stung the nose of the great King.

"You must go to him at once," the Queen Bee said.

"Oh sweeten my honey!" gasped the young Orchid-Bee. "What will he do to me?"

"I don't know," the Queen Bee said. "You'll have to throw yourself on his mercy."

The Orchid-Bee began to fly towards the palace, but not very fast, dawdling as much as he could, thinking that if he took his time, maybe, maybe the King would forget he had sent for him. So he loitered in the magnolia gardens and he lingered in the aster garden. But onward he did fly until suddenly, and much too soon to suit him, he came right to the window of the King's bedroom. And there the King was, waiting for him.

"King Solomon?" the Orchid-Bee buzzed.

"Of course I am King Solomon. Look at my nose and you'll know who I am."

The Orchid-Bee shivered on the windowsill. "Oh yes, Your Majesty, a thousand pardons, Your Majesty . . ."

"Come, come," growled the King. "Why did you bite my Royal Nose?"

The Orchid-Bee hung his head in shame. "Please, Your Majesty, if I may explain?"

"That's what I'm waiting for," King Solomon muttered. "An explanation."

"Well, Your Majesty," the Orchid-Bee stammered. "Here's what happened. I'm a very young Bee, you see, and truly, I just don't know my own strength. I didn't know what could happen with my stingers. I was flying around your bedroom early this morning before you awoke. Believe me, I

96

didn't come with the intention of stinging you. Oh no! I was just flying around and, just as it was beginning to get light, I saw you lying in the bed. And I flew closer for a better look at you."

"You did more than take a look," growled the King.

"Yes, well, I'm coming to that, Your Majesty," the Orchid-Bee said nervously. "You see, I had heard such wonderful stories about the great King Solomon, and I wanted to see you for myself."

He gulped and looked sideways at the King.

The King cleared his throat and said, "Yes? Go on."

"You were sleeping so peacefully," the Orchid-Bee continued. "And before I realized it, I came closer and closer, and then . . . then I saw your beautiful nose!"

The King touched his swollen nose tenderly with his finger-tips.

"I meant to kiss you, dear King," the Orchid-Bee said quickly. "But I got so excited that, instead of kissing you, I stung you! Oh, can you ever forgive me?"

"Well now, well now," King Solomon said gruffly, very much pleased because the Orchid-Bee had meant to kiss him. "Since you are so young and don't know your own strength, I suppose I must forgive you. Yes, I shall. I shall forgive you. I shall forgive you this time, but never let it happen again!"

"Oh no!" exclaimed the Orchid-Bee. "Never, never again. I thank you, dear King, for forgiving me. I thank you very much. And, Your Majesty, because you are so kind to me, some day I shall try to repay you with kindness. Good-bye, dear King. Good-bye."

And the little Orchid-Bee flew out of sight.

The Royal Nose began to get better and, after a few days, all the soreness was gone and the stiffness disappeared and the swelling went down. Soon it looked just as handsome as ever, and King Solomon forgot all about the incident.

Indeed, he soon became too busy to think about such a small and insignificant thing as a Bee, because the Queen of Sheba had come to his court for a visit and King Solomon was so busy answering all the riddles which the Queen of Sheba put to him, that he forgot almost everything, for the time being, except the Queen and her riddles.

One day, just before she departed to return to her own country, she said to him,

"You are indeed the wise King I have heard you were. You have answered every riddle I have put to you, and you have solved every puzzle I have given you. But, O King, I have one more puzzle which I should like to present to you for solution. Are you willing, O Solomon, to unravel one last puzzle?"

King Solomon nodded. "One last puzzle."

The Queen of Sheba clapped her hands and in through the wide double doors leading from the west hall came marching forty beautiful girls. Each girl was dressed in a flowing white gown. Each girl carried a large bouquet of flowers. The girls walked to the east wall and turned and stood facing the Queen of Sheba and King Solomon. The forty girls held their forty bouquets of flowers straight in front of them, at arm's length.

The Queen of Sheba turned to King Solomon.

"Now, Your Majesty," she said slowly, smiling. "Before you stand forty beautiful maidens. Each one carries a bouquet of flowers. Thirty-nine of these bouquets are made of artificial flowers. One bouquet is made of real flowers. Look at them closely. Then tell me, O King, which is the bouquet of real flowers?"

98

King Solomon frowned. Each bouquet looked perfect. It was impossible to tell which were the real flowers, because all the flowers looked exactly alike.

"Let the maidens come a little closer," he commanded.

The Queen of Sheba smiled mischievously. "Oh no, Your Majesty! You cannot win that way. If they came closer, you could smell the flowers. No, no, Your Majesty. You must answer from this distance. Which are the real flowers?"

King Solomon frowned again, knowing that this time he would fail. This time he could not unravel the puzzle presented by the Queen of Sheba. The King frowned in his chagrin and disappointment.

Then, suddenly, from the window behind him, came a little buzzing sound. No one else heard it. It said,

"Bzzzz bzzzzz, Bz Bzzzz. Bz bzzzzz bzzzz bzzz."

The noise was coming from a very young Bee. King Solomon looked at it and recognized the Orchid-Bee who had stung his nose. He was saying,

"Don't worry, O King. I shall help you."

The Bee darted high up towards the ceiling so no one would see him, and then, when he neared the forty beautiful maidens carrying the forty bouquets, he swooped down to the one bouquet which was made of real flowers.

King Solomon rose, turned to the Queen of Sheba, bowed and said,

"Your Majesty, the Queen, the real bouquet is the third from the left."

As the Bee darted up and away from the flowers towards the open window, King Solomon said,

"Bz bzzzz bzzz, bzzzzzz bzz."

"I thank you, friend Bee."

And, laughing gaily, happy that he had repaid King Solomon's kindness, the Orchid-Bee flew out of the window back to the orchid garden.

The Counterfeit Key

The law court of King Solomon was famous. He was known far and wide for his wisdom, and everyone relied on him to be just. People came from all over the kingdom for his decisions.

Now it once happened that, in the city of Lydda, three brothers quarrelled over money. There was no need for the quarrel, because their father had left each of them a large fortune. Just before he died, he had called his three sons, Jonathan and Simon and Ruel, to him, and said,

"The time has come for me to die. I am leaving my vast fortune divided equally amongst the three of you."

"Don't worry about us, father," Jonathan said. "You just get well and enjoy the money yourself."

The father smiled and said, "I cannot get well, and since I cannot, I don't mind going, my sons. I have had a full, rich life. Now I just want to make sure that my fortune is divided equally amongst you."

"We shall do anything you say, father," said Simon.

"Oh indeed, father," Ruel hastened to say. "Your slightest wish will be our command."

"Good," the old man said. "As I said, my money has been divided amongst you. But, in addition, there is something else. Now look over there, in that corner. Do you see that iron chest?"

100

The three sons turned to look at a small iron chest which they had never seen before. When they turned back to their father, they saw that he was smiling, and that in his left hand he held a golden key.

"This key unlocks the chest," the old man said. "That chest is filled with gold coins."

Ruel smiled, and his father said quickly,

"But you must never open that chest unless you are really in great trouble. Now listen to my wish. When I die, I want the chest to go to my oldest son, Jonathan. You are to guard that chest for one year. While it is in your possession, the key shall be in Simon's hands. At the end of the year, the chest shall go to Simon and the key to Ruel. At the end of the second year, the chest shall go to Ruel and the key to Jonathan. Do you understand, my sons?"

Jonathan answered. "Yes, father. It is your wish that the chest and the key shall never be in the possession of the same person."

"To keep any one of us from opening the chest," Simon added.

The old man nodded. "The chest must never be opened unless one of you is in desperate need. When it is opened, all three of you shall divide the gold equally."

"We understand, father," Ruel said softly.

The old man nodded and smiled. He died the next day.

His fortune was divided amongst the three sons. The chest went to Jonathan's house. The key went to Simon. And Ruel began to live the soft and easy life of a rich spendthrift. He paid no attention to his business, but spent his money wildly, buying anything his fancy desired, no matter what the cost. By the time the first year ended, Ruel was penniless.

On the day when the iron treasure-chest was to be sent by Jonathan to Simon's house, and the gold key was to be given to Ruel, the three brothers met at Jonathan's house. Simon handed the gold key to Ruel and said,

"Now you are in possession of the key for one year, Ruel. Take good care of it. Don't lose it."

Ruel looked gloomily at the key in his hand. "Oh, I won't lose it, Simon. But what good is it? I do not have a coin to my name . . ."

Jonathan interrupted him. "You don't have any money, Ruel? What happened to the large fortune our father left you?"

Ruel looked at the ground and scowled and finally he sighed. "I've been unlucky. My business has failed. Everything I tried to do this year went wrong. It's been a sad, unlucky year, and I am penniless."

"Well, that's too bad," Simon said, looking at Jonathan.

Jonathan looked at Simon. They knew what was coming.

"This is the time to open the chest," Ruel said.

Jonathan shook his head. "No. Our father said that the chest should not be opened except in extreme emergency."

"But I am . . ." Ruel started to say.

Jonathan interrupted. "Rather than open the chest, Ruel, I shall give you five hundred gold pieces, and not as a loan, but as a gift. That is a great deal of money. Use it wisely. If you do well in business, you can pay it back, if you wish. If not, consider it a gift."

Ruel's face brightened and he smiled. "Thank you, dear brother. Thank you very much."

Simon went home, taking the chest of gold to keep for one year. Ruel went home, taking Jonathan's gift of five hundred gold pieces, and the gold key.

He liked the look of the key. He liked the feel of it. Often he would study it, wishing he could use it on the lock it would open. When he wasn't day-dreaming about the gold the key could unlock, he was living his life of pleasure. He made no attempt to use Jonathan's gift to revive his business. He used the five hundred gold pieces in banqueting, at the races at King Solomon's Hippodrome, in buying fine clothes. And so, as the second year began to draw to a close, he found he had spent all of his money except five gold pieces.

Two days before the second year ended, Ruel stood in his garden, holding the five gold pieces in one hand and the gold key in the other. He tossed the key up and down, playing with it, frowning at it. Then suddenly, he laughed out loud. He put the five gold pieces in his pouch, left his garden and went to the shop of a goldsmith.

"Make me a duplicate of this key," he said to the goldsmith.

The goldsmith turned the key over and over in his hands.

"Fine key," he said. "I shall make you one just like it for three gold pieces. Out of gold I shall make the key."

"Three gold pieces!" Ruel exclaimed. "Oh no. It doesn't have to be made of gold. Iron is good enough. Make it of iron."

"Very well," the goldsmith said. "It will cost one gold piece. Come back in two weeks . . ."

"Nonsense," Ruel said angrily. "I want it now. Take some iron and hammer it out now, while I wait."

"That will cost you three gold pieces," the goldsmith said. "Because to do this immediately, I shall have to put other important work aside."

"Very well," Ruel growled. "But make it now."

Within an hour, Ruel left the shop, clutching the gold key in his right hand, and in his left hand he carried the counterfeit key of iron.

Two days later the three brothers met at Simon's house. Ruel turned to Jonathan and said,

"I know it is your turn to guard the gold key, and here it is." He showed it to his brothers. "But now, Jonathan and Simon, now we must open the chest and divide the gold. For I confess, I have been extremely unlucky, and I am completely destitute."

Simon frowned. "That is a pity, Ruel. I'm sorry you weren't successful in your business this year. But I shall follow Jonathan's example. Rather than open the chest, I shall give you five hundred gold pieces. If your business prospers and you can repay it, well and good. If not, consider it a gift."

Simon gave Ruel five hundred gold pieces. Ruel gave Jonathan the gold key. Simon gave Ruel the iron chest which he was to guard for one year.

Ruel went home, put the chest away in a safe hiding-place and then for the next year he lived merrily, just like a lord, on the money which Simon had given him, never attempting to work, just enjoying himself, wasting his money and accomplishing nothing.

One day, just as the year was ending, he locked himself in his bedroom, took the iron chest out of hiding, and stood frowning at it. He had no money left. He had spent it all in a year of rich living with nothing to show for it. And this time he did not dare ask either of his brothers for any more gifts. Now he was really in a desperate state and there was no help for him . . . unless he opened the iron chest.

From a very secret and a very safe hiding-place, he took out the counterfeit key which he had made the year before, and with this iron key, he opened the chest. It was filled to the brim with gold coins. Ruel smiled in contentment, scooped out all the coins, stowing them in sacks which he hid most carefully away. Then into the chest he put some stones to make the chest feel as heavy as it had been before. He locked the chest, put it away, went into the garden, dug a hole and in the hole he buried the counterfeit key.

Three days later Jonathan and Simon came to Ruel's house expecting him to meet them with a sad face and complaints. To their surprise, Ruel was smiling brightly.

"Come in, Jonathan. Take a comfortable seat, Simon. And allow me to repay my debts." He gave Jonathan a velvet sack of blue containing five hundred gold pieces, and to Simon a velvet sack of green containing five hundred gold pieces. "I have been very lucky in my business this year, my brothers, and I am happy to repay the loans which you gave me."

The two older brothers congratulated him, never dreaming they were being paid with the gold out of the iron chest.

Ruel then delivered to Jonathan the chest which he was to safeguard for the next year and, of course, Jonathan didn't guess that he would be safe-guarding only a heap of stones. Jonathan gave Simon the gold key to keep for the next year, and the brothers parted happily.

Ruel, now with more money than he ever had had before in his life, really lived recklessly and wildly. He used his money up so fast, it was just like pouring water out onto the earth, and like water it was soaked up. By the end of the year, he had not one gold coin left in his possession.

On the day when the chest was to be given to Simon and the key to Ruel, when the brothers met at Jonathan's house, Ruel confessed to his brothers that he had had an unlucky year. Everything had gone against him and now the time had surely come when they must open the chest. The two older brothers argued long and vainly against Ruel's stubbornness, and finally, Jonathan took the gold key from Simon's hand and opened the chest.

There, instead of gold, were stones! Just plain ordinary stones of the field.

"Stones!" Ruel shouted. "Where is the gold? You have cheated me! My two brothers have cheated me! That's why you would never open the chest before! You stole the gold and cheated me! I want my money!"

Jonathan and Simon, utterly bewildered, looked at each other. They didn't know what to say. Jonathan knew that he was innocent, but perhaps Simon had stolen the gold? Simon knew that he was innocent, but perhaps Jonathan had stolen the gold? And what about Ruel?

A real argument started, with each brother accusing the other, until finally Jonathan put a stop to it.

"Enough. No more quarrelling. One of us has stolen the gold and I know that the guilty man will not just openly admit to his crime. Therefore we shall go to King Solomon. He shall decide which one of us is guilty."

So from Lydda to Jerusalem to the court of Solomon went Jonathan, Simon and Ruel.

When their case was called, Jonathan, as the eldest brother, put the case before the King. He told him of his father's wishes, how the fortune had been divided amongst them, how the chest had travelled from one brother to the other, and how the key had been transferred every year.

Then he concluded, "Now, Your Majesty, we have opened the chest of gold. And in that chest there is no gold. There are only stones."

"One of my brothers stole the gold," Ruel cried.

The King looked thoughtfully at each of the brothers. Jonathan looked embarrassed. Simon looked guilty. And Ruel looked so innocent that he immediately drew the sympathy of the court to him. But King Solomon was not so easily deceived. He thought to himself, one of these three brothers is the thief, but I shall let him betray himself. Aloud he said,

"Your case is difficult indeed. You must give me a little time to think about it. Meanwhile, perhaps you can be of help to me. A puzzling lawsuit was sent to me which I have not yet decided. Since you are businessmen and experienced in the ways of life, perhaps you can help me. So listen carefully.

"This case has come to me from the King of Babylon. In the Babylonian kingdom there was a beautiful maiden who was in love with a handsome young man. They had promised to marry each other; but for some reason, they couldn't marry immediately, and, since they lived in different towns and thus were separated, each was afraid that the other would fall in love with some one else. So they made a promise that neither of them would ever marry anybody else without getting permission from the other."

"Yes, yes," Ruel murmured. "Very wise."

King Solomon continued. "Now the parents of the girl were impatient at the delay in her marriage. They decided that she should marry a different man, a man of their choice. At first the girl was most unhappy and refused even to meet this man, but finally, being an obedient daughter, she did meet him, and, to her surprise, she fell completely in love with him and she wanted to marry him."

"But her promise to the other man?" Simon asked anxiously.

"Yes," the King said. "Her promise to the first man. She remembered it all right and she told the second man that she could not marry him unless the first man gave her his permission. She gathered together a large amount of gold and silver and she and her bridegroom journeyed to the first man's town to talk it over with him. They told him what had happened and asked him to release her from her promise. They offered him the gold and silver as compensation for the broken promise. He refused to take the money. He said he wanted no riches, only the girl's happiness, and if she thought she would be happier with the man whom her parents had selected, then he would release her from the promise."

"A very noble young man," Jonathan said.

"Now hear me," Solomon the King continued. "As the young couple left the young man's village to journey back to their own village, they were halted by a highwayman who wanted to rob the young man not only of his money but of his young bride too. The young man was powerless to protect his young bride, but she spoke up and said to the robber, 'Listen to me, first.' The robber saw no reason not to listen to the girl.

"Thereupon she told him what had happened. 'Now,' she said to the robber. 'If the first man to whom I was engaged acted so nobly and permitted me to marry the man I love, then how can you have the heart to tear me away from this man and to ruin my life?' The robber listened carefully, thought a while, and then let the young couple go free. And, he didn't even steal their money!

"Now," King Solomon said. "This is where I need your help. The King of Babylon has asked me to decide: Who acted most nobly? The young man who gave the girl permission to break her promise, the girl, the man she was going to marry, or the robber? Will you tell me what you think?"

Jonathan and Ruel and Simon all thought carefully, and then Simon spoke up.

"Your Majesty, I believe the girl was the noblest of them all for refusing to break her oath and marry without the permission of her first fiancé."

"Yes, thank you," King Solomon said, turning to Jonathan. "And what is your opinion?"

"Oh," Jonathan answered. "I think the first young man was far nobler than any of the others. He could have demanded that the girl keep her promise and marry him. But even though he loved her very much, he was willing to give up everything so that she could be happy."

"Yes, thank you," King Solomon said, turning to Ruel. "And what is your judgment in this matter?"

Ruel laughed shortly, and said, "There's no doubt about it! The highwayman was the noblest of the three. For look, he wanted to steal the money and the girl. It would have been enough if he had let the girl go free. He still could have stolen the money and no one would have complained. Yes, there's no doubt about it! The highwayman was the noblest of all!"

King Solomon smiled. "Guard!" he commanded. "Arrest that man!"

He pointed to Ruel.

"Here, here!" Ruel protested. "Why do you arrest me?"

"Because you have betrayed your own guilt," the King declared. "You were not impressed by loyalty or honor. All you cared about in the story I told you was who would get the money. Therefore, I say, by your answer you have condemned yourself. You stole Jonathan's and Simon's money!"

At first Ruel tried to protest his innocence. But finally, after much questioning, he broke down and confessed and told the King how he had made a counterfeit key and stolen the gold from the chest.

Ruel went to jail. And everybody left the courtroom marvelling how brilliant King Solomon had been for having told a story about the King of Babylon in order to get a robber in Jerusalem to confess his guilt.

The Tower In The Sea

Far out in the Mediterranean Sea, high up on the balcony of a Tower a beautiful Princess pined in loneliness. She was the daughter of King Solomon, passing her days in fretting in the lonely Tower. Her father had heard rumors that his daughter's fate was to marry an ignorant, old and ugly man from Acco. To save her from this unpleasant fate, the King had shut her away in this Tower in the Sea.

She had only her Lady-in-Waiting for company, and, being so young and gay, it wasn't enough for her, and she was always bored. The only break in the monotony each day was the visit she received from her father's Eagle. He came winging his way every morning across the blue waters, bringing her tempting foods, or a new dress.

This day she leaned against the stone railing of the balcony, looking out over the waves of the Sea. Finally, way off in the distance, she saw a tiny speck. She watched it. It grew larger and larger until soon it was close enough for her to recognize. It was her friend, the Eagle. A few moments later he alighted on the balcony.

"Greetings, O Princess."

"Greetings," she said crossly. "You're late today."

"I know, Your Highness, and I apologize," the Eagle said. "The games at the Hippodrome delayed me. Today is the day for the people of foreign countries to see the races, you know . . ."

"I know," she cried eagerly. "Oh, I should like to be there. Were my father and his court all dressed in light blue? Were the people of Jerusalem dressed in white?"

The Eagle nodded. "Yes, and the people of the surrounding villages wore red, as usual, and those from far away wore green. It was these green-clad people from far away who made me late today, little Princess. Your father sent me to fetch one prince from Persia, and one prince from Egypt."

"Oh, why can't I be there?" cried the Princess. "Instead of in this lonely Tower! I would like to be watching the lads of Gad and Naphtali in their swift races. Oh, it is really all your fault that I'm a prisoner in this Tower."

The Eagle hung his head and sighed. "I know, and I'm sorry. But it was for your own good, Your Highness."

"Tell me again how it happened," the Princess commanded, wanting to keep the Eagle as long as possible. "Tell me again the story of the Canopy of Eagles."

"There are two stories, you remember, Princess," the Eagle said. "One about your grandfather, King David, and one about you. Which shall I tell you first?"

She thought for a moment, then said, "Tell me the one about my grandfather."

The Eagle settled himself firmly on the railing, cleared his throat, and began.

"When King David became very old, the time had come for him to die; but, like all men, of course, he didn't want to die. Now somehow he knew that the Angel of Death had no power to take a man's soul while he was studying the Torah. David knew, too, that he was to die on a Sabbath in his seventieth year. Now from the very day he became seventy, on every Sabbath, he spent every moment diligently studying the Torah so that the Angel of Death could not take his soul. But one Sabbath, David was disturbed by a noise in the garden. When he went to investigate it, and thus stopped his study of the Torah, he found it was the Angel of Death, waiting for his soul. And in the garden, David died.

"It was the Sabbath day and, because it was the Sabbath, your father, now

110

King Solomon, was not permitted to move David's body into the house. This was sad indeed. How could they leave him lying there all day in the hot sun? It wasn't right. It wasn't dignified for a king to lie there exposed. So Solomon summoned me and my eagle-friends and we came and with our wings we formed a revolving canopy as we slowly circled over King David, shielding him from the sun all through the day until the early evening, when the first three stars of the heavens proclaimed that the Sabbath had ended."

The Eagle stopped and the Princess took a deep breath.

"Oh," she said. "That is such a beautiful story. I always like to hear it. Now tell me the other one."

The Eagle cleared his throat again, took another firm grip on the railing and launched into the second story.

"About two moons ago, your father had a trifling quarrel with his friend, Hiram, the King of Tyre. Now as these men do, even a trifling quarrel leads them to war. So King Solomon gathered his army and started to march against the city of Tyre. On the way he came to a broad river, so broad he knew it would take many hours for the army to cross, so they had to pitch their camp on the river-front. The day was hot, very hot. There was no escape from the blazing, blinding sun. King Solomon feared he would lose more men from the heat than in battle. So once again he summoned me and my friends, and all the eagles of the land came and formed a vast canopy over King Solomon's soldiers, shielding them from the hot sun."

"That was very kind of you," the Princess said, "hovering around all day in the hot sun."

"We were happy to serve King Solomon," the Eagle said. "Now one of King Hiram's spies observed all this. He raced off to tell his King, and Hiram was curious to see this Canopy of Eagles. So he came and he was so intrigued by this awning of birds that he and King Solomon just fell into natural, easy conversation and forgot all about the battle they were going to fight."

"That was good," the Princess said.

The Eagle nodded. "So Hiram sat down with the King, right under my wings. I, being the King of the Eagles, of course had spread my protection over the King of Israel. I had taken the place of honor for myself, naturally."

"Naturally." The Princess nodded.

"So of course I was in a position to hear their conversation," the Eagle continued. "And you know how people act when they meet. They say, how are

111

you, and how is your family. And of course, your father and Hiram did too. And then Hiram said, 'And how is the beautiful Princess' . . . meaning you, of course."

"Meaning me, of course." The Princess smiled.

"Well!" exclaimed the Eagle. "The moment he mentioned your name, I remembered I had a very important message for your father. I certainly did not like to interrupt two kings while they were talking. I knew it wasn't polite, to interrupt anybody, of course, and particularly two kings, but, there just wasn't any help for it. So I whispered, 'Ho there, King Solomon, hear me. Ho there, King Solomon.' "

"Oh my!" whispered the Princess. "Was he angry?"

"Well, not angry," said the Eagle. "But stern."

" 'My good Eagle,' he said. 'You are interrupting me and the King of Tyre.' "

" 'A thousand apologies, Your Majesty,' I said, as meekly as I could. 'But I've just remembered that my wife gave me a very important message for you.' "

" 'Very well,' the King said. 'Speak.' "

"So I spoke. I said, 'My wife just returned from an exploratory trip to Acco, Your Majesty, and there she heard two old women say that it has been foretold in the stars that a very poor, very ignorant and very ugly old man from Acco was coming to Jerusalem to marry your daughter.' "

" 'What!' shouted the King, jumping up. 'Never.' "

"Then he quieted down a little and said, 'Of course, it may not be true, but I cannot risk the chance that it is. I shall have to protect my daughter.' "

The Eagle stopped. He and the Princess looked at each other. She sighed. He sighed, and then he said,

"And you know the rest of the story," the Eagle finished weakly. "How he rushed back home and built this Tower in the Sea . . ."

"And imprisoned me in it," the Princess ended gloomily.

They were both silent for a few moments. Then, sighing, she said,

"How I should like to be home. The Queen of Sheba is coming to visit and I'd like to meet her. I'd like to see the beautiful Palace of Glass my father is building for her. I'd like to be dancing in the palace and seeing the races at the Hippodrome. And all I see are the clouds and the stars and the sea."

The Eagle remained silent.

"Well, anyway, dear Eagle," she said. "Thank you for your visit today, and for telling me the two stories. Return now to my father's palace. Tell him I am well but sad. I remain here in the Tower in the Sea."

"At least here you are safe from that unpleasant old man from Acco," the Eagle said, spreading his wings.

And back to Jerusalem he flew.

Now way off in Acco, a young man, handsome and wise, but poor, decided to go out into the world to seek his fortune. He started off merrily, wandering on foot over hills and mountains, crossing rivers and meadows. Usually, night time found him in a village where he could work for his bed and supper.

But by the third week of his wandering, he began to look more and more shabby. And he found it harder to get work in the villages. One day, as night was about to fall, he had the bad luck to be far away from any town. Nowhere for miles could he see shelter of any kind.

"It's the open field for me tonight," he said to himself.

He started walking over the rocky ground, stumbling occasionally on loose stones, beginning to shiver from the cold night air coming down from the mountains.

"If I could only find a piece of sacking to wrap myself in to keep out the cold," he muttered.

And then he found something. It was the carcass of an ox. He looked it over, shuddering. Not a pleasant thing to lie down in, he thought, but it's better than nothing. He settled himself in it and then, because he was so tired, fell immediately asleep.

At that moment, a large bird, flying aloft, looking down to the ground for food, spied the half-eaten carcass of the ox. The bird zoomed downward to the field, scooped up the carcass, with the young man in it, in its powerful claws, soared upward into the sky, flying onwards towards Jerusalem. The sensations of motion awakened the young man. He opened his eyes.

"How close the stars seem to be!" he exclaimed. "Where am I? What, am I moving? Am I dreaming?"

He looked down through a hole in the hide. There, far, far below was the earth. And here he was, high, high up in the sky. The sight dizzied him. He closed his eyes. Then opened them, looked up and saw the huge bird which was carrying him and the carcass. He realized quickly that he'd better be very still because if the bird knew it had captured two prizes, he'd eat the living prey first.

On and on the bird flew. To the young man it seemed like an endless

113

journey. Then, finally, the bird rested its burden on something solid. The young man had no idea where he was. The stars now gave very little light and the moon was hidden behind a cloud. But he felt he was still up somewhere very high, even if it were solid. Cautiously, quietly, he rolled out of the carcass.

And not a moment too soon. The bird lunged and began to devour the hide. When it had eaten all it wanted, it picked up the rest and flew away.

The young man sighed with relief. Now he was safe from that bird. But since he didn't know how high up he was, or where he was, he decided that he'd better remain very still so that he would not roll off this height and dash himself to death.

So there he crouched all night, huddled against the cold — *on the balcony of the Tower in the Sea!*

Inside the Tower, the Princess tossed on her bed, half-wakeful and fretful. At the very first streak of dawn in the sky, she rose, put on her white robe and strode out onto the balcony. She jumped in surprise. There was a bundle of rags on the balcony! Then the bundle of rags stirred and proved to be a man.

"Oh!" she exclaimed. "Who are you? And what are you doing here?"

"Oh, a beautiful Princess," he exclaimed, forgetting his cold and misery at the sight of her.

"Who are you?" she repeated. "And what are you doing on my balcony?"

He rose to his feet and she saw that despite his wretched garments, he was young and tall and handsome. Without speaking, the Princess and the young man from Acco stood looking at each other, falling quickly, silently, deeply in love.

As in a trance, the Princess said, "Oh, you're shivering. Come inside."

She brought him in and as they began to talk, their voices woke the Lady-in-Waiting who rushed in to find the strange young man telling the Princess how the bird had deposited him on her balcony. The Lady-in-Waiting was beside herself with anxiety. Oh, what would the King say when he knew of this man? Oh, what would the King do? She wrung her hands and entreated the young man to leave by the spiral staircase which would take him down to the bottom of the Tower. There the guards would put him in a ship . . .

But the Princess laughed at her, and quieted her. "Don't you worry yourself. My father will not punish you. I shall take full responsibility. Now do be quiet and good."

114

She sent the young man into the next room where he could wash the grime from his face and hands and brush his hair and his clothes. When he was as clean as he could be in his ragged garments, his face shining, his eyes clear and bright, the Princess and he gazed at each other, and together they said,

"My husband."

"My wife."

All through breakfast, they ignored the worries and the entreaties of the Lady-in-Waiting. They didn't even hear her. They looked only at each other, talked only to each other, listened only to each other, as people do who discover they are in love.

After breakfast they went out onto the Balcony to wait for the Eagle. He came early that morning and when he saw a strange man with the Princess, he was so startled, he almost lost his hold on the railing.

"Here, here," he said gruffly. "What have we here?"

"This is my future husband," the Princess said proudly. "This is the man from Acco."

"The man from Acco!" exclaimed the Eagle. "The poor, ignorant, ugly old man from Acco. Oh my wings! His Majesty had better hear about this!"

He wheeled about and flew straight back to Jerusalem. The Eagle returned in less than an hour with King Solomon seated on his right wing. The King began to talk even before he alighted. But the Princess interrupted.

"Please, father. Don't be angry. Please listen to me. This is my true love. This is the man I shall marry."

King Solomon looked at the handsome young man carefully, sternly, then after a moment, he chuckled.

"I can't say he's ugly, can I?" asked the King. "But you are poor, aren't you?" he asked, accusingly.

The young man smiled. "In worldly possessions, Your Majesty, yes. In love, I am rich."

The King started to frown at him; but he liked the look of the man so much, it was hard to keep stern.

"So you have a ready tongue," he said.

The young man bowed. "If his Majesty will permit me, even if I shall sound boastful, may I say that I am neither unskilled nor ignorant. I have been a scholar all my life. I come from an honorable family. I beg of you, Your Majesty, give me your daughter in marriage. We shall be happy together. I know we shall."

King Solomon's great wisdom stood him in good stead now. He was so skilled in reading character, that he knew at a glance that the man standing before him would be a fine husband for the Princess. So, glad that the prediction of the stars was wrong, graciously he gave in at once.

The Eagle carried them all home to Jerusalem, the King and the Lady-in-Waiting on his left wing, the Princess and the Man from Acco on his right. The marriage was held the very next day and the man from Acco and the Princess lived happily ever after.

The Thousand Years' Sleep

One morning when the sun was shining brightly, King Solomon went out into the garden to look for the White Eagle who carried him wherever he wanted to go. He found the Eagle waiting at the river's edge, looking down into the water.

Solomon sat down beside the Eagle. "What do you see in the water?"

"Nothing," said the Eagle. "Just my old face."

Solomon sighed. "Just the same thing. Over and over again. Just the same thing. It's the same face you have seen yesterday. It's the same face you will see tomorrow. Friend Eagle, I am bored today. I want to see something new, something really new, something I have never seen before."

"I have just the thing to show you," said the White Eagle. "Late yesterday afternoon I was at an Eagle-party given by my oldest brother, and every guest was speaking of something new he had seen the day before. My third cousin on my mother's side told us that for the first time in her life she had found the place where the Rainbow is made. If you'd like, I'll take you there."

"Oh no," Solomon said. "That doesn't sound too interesting to me."

"Not interesting!" the Eagle exclaimed. "To see where the Rainbow is made?"

Solomon shook his head.

"Very well," the Eagle said. "Then I shall take you to the place my father's fifth cousin told us about. He has found . . . listen, King Solomon, you'll like this. He has found the secret dwelling of the Four Winds!"

"No," Solomon said, sighing. "Somehow today I don't feel like seeing the secret dwelling of the Four Winds."

117

The White Eagle smiled. "Ah, I can see you're not easily pleased today. Well then, King Solomon, just mount my right wing and I shall show you something which I promise will make your boredom vanish like smoke."

"What is this place?" asked the King.

"I shall not spoil the surprise by telling you," the Eagle said. "I shall call it 'The Enchantment of a Thousand Years.' Actually, it is waiting for you to come to release the spell. But that's all I'll tell you. Just trust in me, Solomon. Just trust in me."

Solomon mounted the right wing of the Eagle without any more discussion, and the big bird soared up, out of the garden, out of the kingdom, and flew on and on to the west. Suddenly he called back,

"We are very close to the place where the Rainbow is born, if you'd like to see it?"

"No," Solomon answered. "Keep going. You promised me the Enchantment of a Thousand Years."

The old Eagle smiled again, and on and on he flew, until suddenly he called back,

"We are very close to the secret hiding-place of the Four Winds, if you'd like to see it?"

"No, no," the King answered. "You promised me the Enchantment of a Thousand Years. Keep going, please."

So on and on the Eagle flew until he came finally to the place he sought. He circled twice to be sure he was right, and then down he zoomed to the foot of a high, high palace made of marble. The Eagle stopped and Solomon alighted.

"What is this magnificent building?" he asked.

"This is the Enchantment of a Thousand Years," the Eagle answered.

"How I should like to go inside!" Solomon exclaimed. "I want to see this palace. Where is the entrance?"

"That I do not know," the Eagle said. "I brought you here. The rest is for you to do. I shall wait for you here, by this little silvery brook where I may quench my thirst while you are searching."

Solomon started off on foot along a path made of green marble. The path went round and round the building, but no matter where the King looked, he saw neither a door nor a window by which he could enter. The more he

118

walked, the more curious he became. With every step he became more determined to get into this palace and see it for himself.

Once more he walked around the green marble path until suddenly he
saw hidden under some low hanging vines a yellow marble staircase leading
up. He stooped under the vines until he had started up the yellow marble
staircase. Then he straightened, and up and up he walked until he thought
he could not walk any farther. He stopped for a moment to rest and then, to
his surprise, he noticed that he had stopped at the nest of an old eagle.

"How do you do, Friend Eagle," Solomon said. "I am looking for a way
into this palace. Perhaps you can tell me where I shall find a door."

The Eagle shook his head. "Ah," he said sadly. "I am too young to have
gained such knowledge. I am only seven hundred years old."

"Seven hundred years old and you do not know where the entrance is!"
King Solomon exclaimed.

"No," the Eagle said and sighed. "But just keep on walking up these five
hundred stairs, much higher, you will find my brother's nest. He is older
than I. He is nine hundred years old. Perhaps he will be able to give you the
answer."

"Then I shall go and find your brother," Solomon said. "Thank you very
much."

As he began to walk away from the Eagle who was only seven hundred
years old, he saw that now the stairs were made of green marble. He began
climbing these steps, and on and on he walked. Farther and farther up he
went until he felt he couldn't go one more step. He stopped to rest. And just
where he stopped, he saw an Eagle's nest.

"Ho there, Friend Eagle," he called.

Up from the nest popped a big Eagle who looked with great curiosity
at this man who had climbed so high, and the man looked with great curiosity
at this bird who was so old.

"Are you really nine hundred years old?" Solomon asked the Eagle.

"I am. But how did you know?" the Eagle asked in turn.

"Your brother told me," Solomon said.

"Yes, it is true. I am nine hundred years old. But what are you doing up
here so high? Did you fly?"

Solomon laughed. "No, I am not a bird like you. I have *walked* up these

119

steps looking for a door. I want to go into this palace. Do you know where the door is?"

"Ah, let me think." The Eagle closed his eyes and thought. Then he opened his eyes, shaking his head. "It seems to me I knew once, but if I did know, I've forgotten."

"What a pity!" King Solomon exclaimed. "I would like to go into the palace. Please try to remember."

"Well, I can't," the Eagle said. "I've tried but I just don't remember. But my older brother . . ."

"Your older brother!" Solomon exclaimed.

"Yes," said the Eagle. "I have a brother who is thirteen hundred years old. His nest is up yonder, at the top of those five hundred marble steps. Just you go up and ask him. I'm sure he'll know."

So the King left the nine hundred-year-old Eagle and began to climb the five hundred marble steps. He climbed and climbed for a long, long time until he felt he must surely be reaching the clouds. Then finally he came to the last step, and there, right at the top was an Eagle's nest.

The King looked into the nest and saw a very, very old Eagle who opened his eyes and said in a very faint voice,

"What seek ye?"

"Can you tell me where to find the door into this palace?" Solomon asked most respectfully, since this Eagle was thirteen hundred years old.

"Let me think, let me think," the old Eagle said, and then, without hurry, he continued. "Oh yes, I remember hearing my father tell me once that there is a door. It is on the west side. But it's all covered with dust and perhaps you will not find it."

Solomon thanked him, said good-bye, turned west and walked all the way down the stairs and around to the west side of the old castle. But he couldn't find a door. The whole wall was covered with thick dust, the dust of the ages.

He found a branch of a tree and with it began to sweep the dust off the west wall until, suddenly, he found it! It was an old iron door. He wiped away the last of the dust and there saw an inscription on the door. It was in a strange language, but since Solomon was so wise and knew all languages, he was able to guess at it from the languages he knew. The inscription read:—

"We who live in this palace lived for a long time in great luxury. Then

120

we lost our wealth and, when we could no longer find food to eat, we ground pearls into flour instead of wheat, but we could not eat pearl-flour and we are about to die. Before we die, we bequeath this palace to the Eagles."

After reading the inscription, Solomon was more curious than ever to go into the palace, but he could not open the door. Then, examining it more closely, he saw a second inscription which told him to lift the second stone off the right hand edge of the door, and there he would find the key.

He did as directed, and found a long iron key. This he fitted into the lock, and, using both hands, slowly, slowly he was able to move the key. It turned with a great groaning sound. Slowly, slowly he turned the round iron ring-knob and, creaking and groaning, inch by inch the door opened inward.

And Solomon stepped inside the palace.

He found himself in a marble hallway, facing three doors. The first door was cast in ivory and on it in gold gleamed the words:

O man, do not let time deceive you. You must wither away and
find your home in the arms of the earth.

The King walked to the second door which was cast in silver and in letters written in pearls, he read:

Do not waste your life in speedy action. Move slowly. For when
you are finished with life, the world belongs to others.

Then to the third door, cast in gold, with letters written in ruby, the King read the message inscribed there:

No man remains on earth forever. No man knows the day of
his departure.

Solomon opened the golden door and stepped into a vast room, rich in appearance. The floors were made of gold, and the walls were made of pearls. But more astonishing, everywhere he looked, he saw statues. The statues lined every wall and even in the middle of the room. Solomon walked from statue to statue and soon came upon one which looked as if it were alive!

Suddenly, from out of the throat of this statue came words!

"Man, son of man, who art thou?"

"I am Solomon, King of Israel."

"Welcome, O Solomon, King of Israel!" The statue spoke again. "For one thousand years, I and my subjects have awaited thy coming. Read,

read the inscription engraved on my collar, O Solomon. Release me and my subjects from this thousand-year enchantment."

Then the statue fell silent and nothing more that Solomon said to it could bring forth more speech. Solomon looked carefully around this vast audience chamber. At one end stood a large banqueting table and seated at the table were many statues, perhaps twenty, overtaken by some strange spell as they had sat at their meal. All over the room, in gold chairs, in silver chairs, wherever those people who lived here a thousand years ago happened to be when the spell was cast, there they remained, turned to stone. The

statue which had seemed alive and had spoken stood on a pedestal made of rubies and precious stones.

The King walked close to this statue and saw that on its collar there was a silver plate. There was writing on the silver plate. He pulled it off and read the inscription:

> I, Shadad ben Ad, ruled over a thousand-thousand provinces,
> rode on a thousand-thousand horses, had a thousand-thousand
> kings loyal to me, vanquished in battle a thousand-thousand
> warriors. Yet, powerful though I was, when the Angel of Death
> came to gather my soul, I was powerless against him.

For a moment King Solomon stood speechless, gazing around at this vast room. For one thousand years the spell had lasted. These statues had been waiting for him, Solomon, King of Israel, to release the spell. He stood straight now, and spoke the one word which could break the enchantment of a thousand years. Loudly, clearly, Solomon pronounced the Divine Name.

As the last syllable left his lips, slowly, with a gentle crunching sound, all the statues began to crumble before his eyes until each statue became a heap of white dust. The pearl walls crumbled too and became a fine, white dust. The golden floors began to crumble and, as the floors crumbled, Solomon felt himself sliding, sliding, downward, downward, until finally, his mouth filled with white dust and his hair covered with the brown dust of the crumbling floors, he found himself at the bottom, at the first step leading to the palace where he had left his Eagle.

As Solomon rose to his feet, he turned backward to look at the magnificent palace which he had found and which now lay in a huge mound as a heap of white ashes.

"You broke the enchantment of a thousand years," the Eagle said. "It was for this that these statues had been waiting."

As Solomon mounted the wing of the Eagle to begin his homeward journey, he looked once more at the high hill of fine dust and said,

"Dust thou art, to dust returneth."

Namalah And The Magic Carpet

King Solomon had more good fortune than any man has ever had in the whole world. He was a mighty king. He possessed vast wealth. God had given him great wisdom. He owned the wonderful ring with the seal which had engraved on it the Almighty Name and therefore gave him great powers. He had control over the demons. The animals were all his friends and did everything he commanded them to do.

So, little by little, this wonderful King became more and more haughty, more and more vain, until he was in danger of losing his wisdom and becoming arrogant beyond control. Then finally he came into the possession of one more thing which added to his power and fed his vanity.

He became the owner of a huge piece of tapestry. It was acres in length and acres in width and was made of green silk interwoven with pure gold. It became known as Solomon's Magic Carpet.

Whenever Solomon seated himself on it, it would waft him through the air, wherever he wanted to go. He could have breakfast in Damascus and supper in Media, and all he had to do was to sit on a piece of carpet.

One day he decided to go for a little ride on the magic carpet. He ordered Benaiah to come with him, and his Royal Scribe, in case he should want to dictate a Proverb or two, and also one thousand soldiers. It made quite a crowd. As soon as everyone was on it, with the King seated in the center, he clapped his hands and ordered,

"Rise! To Damascus!"

The Tapestry rose from the ground as easily as though it were holding six feathers, and smoothly and gently began to sail through the air. The soldiers had never been on this magic carpet, they had never been off the ground, and they were full of excitement to be sailing through the air as though they were birds. But King Solomon sat serenely in the very center. He was used to such magic. He had flown many times on the wings of his great Eagle and on this carpet, and, truth to tell, he wasn't excited at all. He had everything he wanted. He had seen everything he wanted to see. Everything came too easily to him. There was no surprise and no mystery left in the world for him to discover. And he was bored.

He sat in the center of the Magic Tapestry thinking how powerful and wonderful he was. There was no one as brilliant, as rich, as all-knowing as he. And suddenly he exclaimed aloud,

"There is no one like me in the world!"

Benaiah stared at him. Never before had he heard King Solomon boast.

"No," Solomon repeated. "There is none like me in the whole world. God has given me wisdom, wealth, power, besides making me the ruler of many lands."

As he said those words, the North Wind, in huge gusts, came blasting along and with such force that it seemed as if the Wind were angry. It swept the thousand soldiers right off the Magic Tapestry into the arms of the South Wind which began to pull them down towards the earth. And the North

Wind continued to blow, threatening to sweep Benaiah and the Royal Scribe and the King right after the soldiers!

"Cease this blowing and this blasting and this sweeping!" the King ordered.

But the North Wind blew once more, and said angrily, "I will not cease this blowing and this blasting and this sweeping."

"Cease, I say," commanded the King. "And return my soldiers to me!"

"Oh no," the North Wind said. "Not while you are so haughty. Not while you are so proud. I heard what you said to Benaiah. You have forgotten God in your stubborn pride."

"I, forget God!" exclaimed Solomon. "I did not forget Him. If you heard me speak to Benaiah, then you know that I said that God had given me my wisdom and my power and made me the ruler of the world."

"Yes, yes," the North Wind said, blowing angrily. "You said those words, but in your heart you were thinking that you could have done all that without God's help."

The King stared for a moment, then said, "You are right, North Wind. Those were my very thoughts. You are right to chide me for being haughty and proud. Return my soldiers to me and I shall be modest and humble once more."

"Very well," the North Wind said grumpily, then shouted, "Return!" to the South Wind, who altered his course, turned in mid-air, and lifted all the soldiers right back on the Tapestry.

Then the Winds blew away, and all was quiet and serene once more. But the thousand soldiers were green in the face from their fright at having been blown off the Tapestry. And their Captain begged the King to return them to Jerusalem.

"Why?" asked the King. "The soldiers are no longer in danger. Besides, not one was lost or hurt."

"Still," begged the Captain. "They want to return."

"Very well." King Solomon clapped his hands and gave this order to the Magic Tapestry. "Return, O Carpet, to Jerusalem!"

Slowly it banked, tilted slightly, made a slow, cautious turn, and headed back towards home.

The King had learned his lesson and, for a few days, he was neither haughty nor proud, but listened to the opinions of other people, consulted

126

others on things which he wished to do. He was tame, very tame for a few days. Then, one morning he woke full of spirit and decided to take a little ride. But this time he would go alone.

He seated himself in the center of the Magic Carpet, clapped his hands, and said,

"Rise! Journey without destination!"

The Magic Tapestry rose gently in the air and soon was wafting along amongst the clouds. The King rode high above the earth, enjoying himself, feeling at peace with the world.

Soon they crossed two mountains. Deep between them was a green and peaceful-looking valley. The King clapped his hands and ordered,

"Return! Descend into this valley!"

Slowly, gently, the Magic Tapestry wafted down until it rested the King right in the center of the valley. He rose from the carpet and began to explore, not noticing that he had stepped into a village of Ants who were dashing to and fro on their many little tasks. When the King began stamping about in his big and heavy boots, the Ants tried to scurry away, shrieking in fright.

The King, who understood the language of every living thing, heard this shrill squeaking. He stopped walking, looked down, and listened.

"Stop! Stop!" a strong Ant voice called. "Stop in your tracks or you will all be murdered by King Solomon!"

"Here! Here!" commanded the King. "Who gave this order?"

"I, Namalah, the Queen of the Ants."

"Why did you order the ants to stop work?" King Solomon asked. "And why do you accuse me of murder?"

"Because," said the Queen of the Ants in her squeaky voice. "You would destroy us all within a few minutes with your big, clumsy feet."

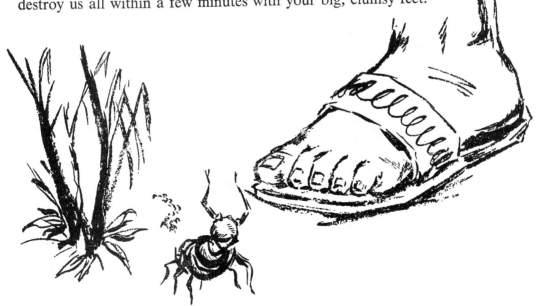

"Is that the way to talk to the King?" Solomon asked.

"Is that the way to treat the Queen?" Queen Namalah retorted. "Look at your feet. Aren't they big? They could crush hundreds of my subjects with one step."

Solomon looked down at his feet. They had never seemed really big before, but now he realized that hundreds of ants could fit into the space occupied by one foot and that he could crush them all.

"You are quite right," he said to the Queen. "And I apologize. I did not realize I had blundered into your village. I did not realize what harm I could cause."

"Well, of course," the Queen said. "I realize you didn't do it on purpose."

King Solomon looked behind him. There was a clear space of ground. It was empty. No ants were crawling there. He stepped backward into that clear space. Then he said to the Queen of Ants,

"Now I have stepped away and your subjects are safe from my big boots."

"Thank you very much," the Queen said graciously. "That was indeed an anxious few moments you put us through."

"I am truly sorry," the King said. "And now, if you are over your fright, may I ask you one question?"

"I will answer it," the Queen said haughtily. "Pick me up and place me on your hand."

King Solomon stooped, reached over, picked up the Ant-Queen and placed her on the palm of his left hand.

"There now. There you are on my hand. Now will you answer my question?"

"Ask your question," she said.

"Tell me, O Queen of the Ants. Is there any one greater than I in the whole world?"

The Queen looked at him for a moment, raised her little head, and said scornfully,

"Yes."

"Yes!" exclaimed the King. "Did you say yes?"

"I did," the Queen answered.

Solomon looked sternly at the Ant and then said, "So you think there is someone greater than I. Let me hear you say it. Who is that person?"

"I," said the Queen.

"You?" the King asked, astonished. "You, a little Ant? Indeed. How are you greater than I, Solomon, King of Israel?"

"If I were not greater than you," the Ant replied calmly, "God would not have led me here and put me on your hand."

"Nonsense," the King muttered. "Don't you really realize who I am? I am Solomon, the son of David. I am Solomon, King of Israel. I am Solomon, the wisest of all men."

"Yes," the Queen of Ants said. "I know who you are. But even if you are the son of David, even if you are the King of Israel, there is no need for you to be so proud. There is no need for you to be so haughty."

"Proud. Haughty," the King murmured. "You are right. I had forgotten again. It is so easy to forget. I must practise constantly. I must learn and keep learning to be modest. I must try and try again to be humble."

He put the Queen of Ants back into the ant village. "I thank you, O Queen," he said. "For this lesson you have given me. And now, farewell."

"Farewell, O King," the Queen of the Ants said. "May you always be courageous in action but humble in spirit."

The King lifted his hand in salute, seated himself in the center of the Magic Tapestry, and said,

"Rise, O Carpet. Return me to my palace."

As the Magic Tapestry rose into the air, the King said,

"I thank you, too, Magic Tapestry. On the travels you have taken me, I have learned new wisdom. I have learned from the strong and powerful winds, and through the small and humble ant. All that a man is, all that a man has, comes from God. No one has the right to be proud. No one has the right to be haughty. But every man should be grateful for his gifts and use them wisely and well."

The Man Who Laughed

King Solomon had a friend named Asher who lived far from Jerusalem. Every spring he travelled the long distance from his home just to visit the King. He would stay there at the palace for several days, enjoying the King's company, learning as much wisdom from Solomon as he could absorb in that short time.

When his visit ended and he prepared to leave for home, the King never let him go away empty-handed. He always gave him a gift. One year the gift was a fine pearl for Asher's wife. Another year he was given a beautiful horse which the King had bought in Arabia.

The next time when Asher came to King Solomon's court for his usual visit, when he prepared to leave, he said to the King,

"Please, Your Majesty, I know that as always you are preparing to give me a gift as I depart."

"Indeed," the King answered. "I have something especially fine to give you this year."

"I am very grateful, Your Majesty," Asher said. "But may I be bold enough this time to ask for a gift of my own choosing?"

"Well, of course," King Solomon said, though this was quite unusual. "What is it that you'd like to have, Asher?"

"Please, Your Majesty," Asher said a trifle timidly. "Would you give me a little of your knowledge about animals? I do not ask that you teach me how to *talk* to animals, only that you teach me how to listen to them and to understand what they say."

The King frowned. "Now you ask something difficult of me, Asher. I can easily teach you how to understand everything the animals say, but I hesitate to do so because, there is one big danger involved in it."

"What is that danger?" Asher asked.

"There is a terrible danger," the King answered. "The danger of death itself. Hear me, my friend. If I were to teach you how to understand the language of animals, and if you ever told any person, any person at all that you possess that knowledge, you would die immediately!"

130

"Indeed. I had no idea that it was that dangerous." Asher stared at the King's crown, thinking deeply. "Why would I die if I told anybody that I understand the language of animals, if I did?"

"I don't know why," the King said. "But so it is. In fact, it is only my magic ring which protects me. There is no protection for you. But, I am willing to teach you. Are you willing to take the risk?"

Asher said quickly, "Yes, Your Majesty. I do not believe I would ever be in real danger. I am a quiet person. I do not babble everything I know. And certainly if my life depended on not telling, you may rest assured, I would keep silent."

"Very well, then," the King said. "I shall give you the gift of this special knowledge. I shall teach you how to understand the language of the animals."

And he did.

And on his journey back to his home, Asher was overjoyed because everything he saw on the road, crossing the rivers, climbing the mountains became much more interesting to him because he could understand what every animal he met had to say. He heard a Rabbit scolding his wife, and Asher walked on, chuckling to himself. He heard an Owl complaining because it was awakened during the daytime. And Asher walked on, chuckling to himself. He heard a Bluejay and a Robin quarrelling high up in the branches of a tree. Everything amused Asher now that he could translate the speech of the animals he encountered, and so his journey back seemed so much shorter than it had ever been.

When he reached his home, as usual, he had to tell his wife everything that he had seen and heard at King Solomon's court. He told her all about the new fashions worn by the ladies of the court this season. He described the horseraces at the Hippodrome, and the various entertainments at the Palace. He told her about the many law suits which he had heard King Solomon decide. He remembered to tell her every single detail of everything he had seen or heard. Except, of course, he did not tell her that he now possessed the strange and unusual power of understanding the language of animals.

His life resumed its usual pattern and day followed day. Always a happy man, Asher now was happier than he had ever been. There was so much more interest in his life. He had the animals to amuse him now. He would hear their arguments and their quarrels and even their jokes, and he frequently laughed or chuckled at his work. It made his wife curious to see him laughing so often, particularly when *she* could never see anything funny to laugh at.

One day, Asher was busy in the barn, preparing the food for his work animals. The Ox and the Donkey were in stalls next to each other. As Asher piled the hay and corn for the Ox in its stall, he heard the Donkey say,

"Tell me, Brother Ox, how are you coming along? Do these people treat you well or badly?"

"Ah, Brother Donkey," sighed the Ox. "If I could only tell you."

"You may tell me," the Donkey said. "I won't tell anybody else."

"Promise?" the Ox asked, and when the Donkey brayed his promise, the Ox said, "My life is hard, very hard. Listen to me, Brother Donkey. Day and night I work and work. I work so hard that, I declare, I don't know what I'm going to do."

"Oh, that's too bad," the Donkey said. "I'll tell you what, Brother Ox. I'm not surprised at what you tell me. I have watched how hard you work, and I have been sorry for you. And now I have thought of a good scheme to help you."

"Oh, you are a kind and good friend," the Ox said. "Quickly, tell me. What is your plan?"

"If you will follow my advice," the Donkey said, "you can do only half the amount of work you do now. Why, really, it's possible for you to live at great leisure."

"Well, tell me," implored the Ox.

"Listen." The Donkey looked all around to see that no one was listening, but there was only their owner, Asher himself, and the Donkey thought he couldn't understand, so he said,

"Now believe me, Friend Ox, there is nothing I want for myself, you understand that. I am trying to help you only out of the goodness of my heart. Now this is my advice. Do not eat your supper tonight. Don't touch the straw. Don't take a bite of the hay. Then our master will think you are sick, and he will not send you out to the field to work tomorrow, and you will have a good rest. Hee haw, that's exactly what I did today, hee haw."

Asher, of course, didn't show by even a flicker of the eyelash that he had heard or understood. He heard the Ox low, as usual, and the Donkey bray, but he pretended that all he heard were just the usual barnyard noises. He

132

left the stable, intending to return after dark, to see what the Donkey's game was.

Meanwhile, the Ox, thinking the Donkey meant to do him a favor, did as he had been advised, and refused to eat his supper that night. There it remained, the straw and the hay, temptingly piled near the Ox, but he didn't eat it.

As soon as it got dark, Asher crept out of the house, and went to the barns. There he found all the animals asleep, except the Donkey. The Ox was asleep, hungry though he was. And while Asher watched, the Donkey, whispering happy hee-haws to himself, ate up the Ox's supper.

Asher controlled himself until he was back in the kitchen of his house and then, thinking of the smart trick the Donkey had played on the Ox, he began to laugh. And he laughed and he laughed. His wife, seeing nothing to laugh about, said,

"Now, Asher, what is so funny? Come, tell me. I like to laugh too."

Asher, controlling his laughter with difficulty, remembering King Solomon's advice not to tell anyone his secret, just shook his head, and said,

"It was nothing, nothing at all, just something I happened to think of."

His wife wasn't satisfied, but Asher refused to explain any further. When he went to bed that night, he decided he would have to punish the Donkey for the trick he had played on the Ox.

Early the next morning, he went out to the barn to the Ox's stall. Stroking the Ox on the neck, he said gently,

"Poor Ox, you must be very sick. You didn't eat your supper last night. I shall let you rest today, you poor beast."

"Hey," the Donkey yelled from his stall to the Ox. "You did eat your supper! The food is all gone!"

"I know the food is gone," the Ox called back. "But I didn't eat it. I don't know what happened to it. But that was splendid advice you gave me, Friend Donkey. Our master is letting me rest today."

Then Asher walked over to the stall of the Donkey and to the servant standing there, he gave an order.

"Let the Donkey work all day today and all night tonight. The Donkey had a rest-day yesterday, and besides, he ate his portion of supper and the Ox's portion, so he ought to be able to do his work and the Ox's too."

And so the Donkey was fairly caught in his own trick!

That evening, when the animals were brought to the stables for their supper, Asher was there, waiting for the Donkey to be brought in for his meal. The usual hay and straw were put into the Ox's stall, but he wasn't eating any of it yet. He wanted to ask the Donkey's advice again. Yesterday his advice had been so good.

Soon the Donkey came stumbling into the barn, dragging his hooves, his head hanging, the very picture of weariness. Asher heard the Ox call out,

"Ho there, Friend Donkey. What did you hear out in the fields today?"

The Donkey, furious for having to do the Ox's work as well as his own, said spitefully,

"I heard our master talking to his servant. They decided that if you didn't eat your supper tonight, they would slaughter you for their food."

"Slaughter me!" squealed the Ox. "Oh, how dreadful!"

He plunged his head down into the hay and began to eat as though he hadn't a moment to lose.

Asher began to laugh. He walked back to the house, laughing so hard he could not control himself. And now his wife became very impatient.

"Really, it seems to me that nowadays you are always laughing. And I do declare, I see nothing to laugh about. You must tell me what the joke is."

"Oh, it's nothing, really," Asher said, trying to stifle his laughter. "Just something I happened to think of."

"No," said his wife. "This time you cannot put me off. I insist on knowing what you find so funny. Now Asher, listen to me. If you don't tell me, I shall leave this house this instant and never return!"

That statement sobered Asher quickly and he stopped laughing. He realized that he faced a serious problem. He dearly loved his wife and did not want her to leave. If he did not tell her why he laughed, she would leave him! If he told her why, he would die! Well, he thought, he could not bear to live without his wife, so he decided to tell her.

"Give me one hour," he said to her. "At the end of the hour, I shall tell you why I laughed."

"Very well," agreed his wife.

He went out into the farmyard. He had made the decision to die and he wanted to look over everything he loved one last time.

Now his favorite dog somehow guessed, as dogs often do who love their master, that his master's life was threatened, and perhaps was going to end.

He became so sad that he could not eat his supper. But the Rooster, shooing all the hens who were his wives away from him, ate up his supper and theirs too and even the dog's, since he refused to touch it. This angered the Dog, and he said,

"You unfeeling Rooster! You impudent Rooster! Our master is going to die and all you can do is to enjoy yourself as at a banquet!"

The Rooster lifted his head from the dish out of which he was eating and laughed. "Listen, Brother Dog, why should I suffer just because our master is a fool?"

"How dare you call our master a fool!" the Dog shouted, and barked loudly.

"Of course he's a fool," the Rooster said. "I happen to know what the trouble is. His wife insists that he tell her his secret. If he tells her, he will die. Now isn't it silly for him to die just because he can't keep a secret? Now look at me. I have many wives, and *I* am their master. They do what I say. I wouldn't be fool enough to die just because I couldn't rule my wife. Our master has only one wife and that one he cannot control or manage. Therefore I say he is a fool."

Asher walked away from the Dog and the Rooster, thinking, of course the Rooster is quite right. I should not forfeit my life. I shall not tell my wife my secret. I shall not die, but live.

He went back into the kitchen where his wife was waiting, and he said,

"Listen to me, my wife. Whenever you see me laughing, I laugh because I have a secret. Now, if I tell you this secret, I shall die. My life is in your hands. What do you wish? Do you wish to know the secret? Or do you wish me to live?"

"Oh!" The wife jumped up from her chair. "Oh, Asher, I want you to live. I want you to live. Keep your secret. I don't ever want to know it! I want you to live!"

And so Asher went on living, a long and full and happy life. The gift of King Solomon, to understand the language of the animals, remained with him always. Every day brought him new pleasures and he grew round and fat, chuckling over the interesting and amusing conversations he heard amongst the animals. Often his wife looked at him in surprise, but she held her tongue and shook her head, smiling at her husband, glad that he enjoyed his life so much.

The King's Pawn

King Solomon had many amusements. He enjoyed riding a horse and watching the horse races at the Hippodrome. He liked to listen to music and to watch dancing. It interested him to fly about the world either on his Magic Tapestry or on the wing of his friendly Eagle.

But perhaps best of all he liked to play chess. And his favorite opponent was Benaiah who, next to the King, held the highest position in the court. While Benaiah was a very wise man, and while he played a very good game of chess, still he was not as good as Solomon, and the King won every single

136

game they ever played. And Benaiah, though never admitting it, of course, wanted nothing more than to win a game from the King, just once.

One day Benaiah had gone down to the dungeons. The demon Asmodeus had been insisting on seeing him. As soon as Benaiah opened the heavy stone door, Asmodeus began talking.

"See here, Benaiah. You captured me for King Solomon. So it's up to you to see that he keeps his promise. He said that if I helped him find the Shamir worm, he'd release me. I helped him find the Shamir worm — and look at me, still bound in chains."

"I'll remind the King of his promise," Benaiah said.

"When?" demanded Asmodeus.

"Now," answered Benaiah. "I was just on my way to our evening chess game."

"Then why do you look so gloomy?" Asmodeus asked. "Here you are, a favorite of the King, his chess partner. All you have to do is to play a game with Solomon, a game of chess, and you look as if you'd lost your last friend."

"Because I never win," Benaiah burst out. "I never, never win. Oh, I'd give my soul to win one game of chess!"

"You would?" Asmodeus asked slyly.

Benaiah calmed down and said coldly. "Of course not. I was talking wildly. But I would like to win one game, just one."

"Then how about a little cheating?" Asmodeus chuckled.

"Cheating!" Benaiah said indignantly. "Never. Enough of this conversation."

He turned to the door, and Asmodeus said softly, "You could win by hook or by crook."

Asmodeus laughed softly, a low demonish laugh. Benaiah closed the door angrily and strode away up the stone steps to the palace, with Asmodeus' words ringing in his head, over and over,

"I could win by hook or by crook."

That evening, after the meal, Solomon and Benaiah, as usual, were playing their after-supper chess game. The King had just moved the bishop when the game was interrupted. Solomon was summoned from the room by his mother Bathsheba. Left alone Benaiah was studying the chess board. He saw that the King, by the move he had just made with the bishop, would win the game. An uncontrollable rage took possession of Benaiah.

Why couldn't he win a single game from the King? It was intolerable. He couldn't stand it. He *must* win a game, at least one game.

All of a sudden, Benaiah saw the dungeon scene in Asmodeus' cell. He heard Asmodeus chuckle. He saw Asmodeus smile. He heard Asmodeus say,

"Win, win by hook or by crook."

Benaiah whispered to himself, "I can't cheat. I cannot."

Then again came the ghost of Asmodeus' voice: "By hook or by crook."

And to himself Benaiah murmured, "By hook or by crook."

Almost as if he didn't know what he was doing, Benaiah reached over and moved the King's knight in such a way that he, Benaiah, would easily win this game.

Then he leaned back and closed his eyes. He pretended to be taking a nap.

The King returned in a few moments. Benaiah opened his eyes and sat up, prepared to go on with the game. Inwardly he was shivering because he had cheated. He pretended to be absorbed in the chess pieces so he didn't have to look at Solomon. But the moment the King looked at the chess board, he knew that Benaiah had moved the knight, because Solomon remembered the position of every piece on the board, both his and Benaiah's. But he said nothing, and let the game go on to the end. He said nothing even when Benaiah won the game. He just smiled and then congratulated Benaiah on winning his first game of chess.

But, when they parted for the night, the King could not sleep. He didn't like it that the honest Benaiah had for the first time resorted to trickery. Benaiah has never cheated before, he said to himself. I shall have to punish him somehow. I must let Benaiah know that I know he cheated me. I cannot permit the sin to be successful. But I will not accuse him in public and shame him. I must find a way to make him confess.

Then, that very night, something occurred which gave Solomon the opportunity he sought to make Benaiah confess his sin of cheating.

Because he was so restless, Solomon decided to go outdoors. Perhaps a stroll in the open air would calm him down and make him sleep. He found some clothes belonging to one of his servants, dressed in them, and slipped out the palace gate into the night. He stopped for a moment to let his eyes get accustomed to the darkness. As he waited, he heard someone whispering.

"Here is the palace," a rough voice whispered. "What valuable things there are behind those walls. If we could only get in there and steal some of those treasures, ah, we could be rich for life."

138

"Oh, to be rich for life!" the other voice whispered. "Do you think we could get in? How could we break into the palace?"

King Solomon whistled in the direction of the voices.

"Hsst! Listen to me! I can help you get into the palace."

"Who goes there?" called one of the thieves in alarm.

They both held up hooded lanterns. Solomon strolled over to them so they could see him clearly in their light. He didn't try to hide himself. When they would see his rough clothes, they would think he was one of them. Coming close he whispered,

"I'm just another thief like yourself. I, too, would like to steal into the palace and get some of the King's treasures. And I know just how we can do it."

"How?" the second thief whispered.

"Not so fast," Solomon said. "First we must make a pledge that we will divide all our loot equally amongst the three of us."

The first thief sneered. "First we must get the loot."

The second thief laughed hoarsely. "No, first we must get into the palace."

"Oh that's easy," said Solomon. "Look." He held up his hand and both the thieves saw him holding a key. "I have a key to the gate!"

"Oho," whistled the second thief. "A key. That's an easy way to get in all right."

"Right enough," the first thief said. "I'll agree to dividing the loot evenly."

"So will I," the second thief said quickly.

"Agreed," whispered Solomon. "Just follow me."

The thieves hid their lanterns behind a tree after extinguishing the flames. Solomon led the way, opening the gate with his key, and the three of them stole into the palace. Solomon led them into the treasure room.

"Wait here," he whispered hoarsely. "Here by the door. I know where to find the key to the treasure chests. I shall be back in one minute."

Under cover of the darkness, Solomon crept away to his own bedroom, where he changed out of the rough clothes back into his own. Then he called his guard and said,

"Go to the treasure room in the north hall. There you will find two thieves. Arrest them."

The Guard hurried away to obey the order. He returned in a very short time to say that the thieves were safely in jail. Solomon dismissed the Guard and went smiling to bed. Soon he was sound asleep.

Early the next morning, after breakfast, King Solomon, together with his entourage, the Royal Clerk, the Royal Secretary, and his Guards, went to the Sanhedrin. This was the highest court in the land and it was in session that morning. Benaiah was the President of the Sanhedrin, so he was the presiding judge.

The whole court rose when Solomon, the King, entered the room.

"Your Majesty!" Benaiah exclaimed. "The Sanhedrin is honored with your presence. But let us hear, O King, why you come to this court."

The King bowed, and the seventy members of the court resumed their seats. Then Solomon turned to Benaiah and said,

"Your Honor, I come on a most simple matter. I wish this court to tell me the answer to this question: What punishment should be given to a thief?"

Benaiah looked bewildered. The King had brought no prisoners into the courtroom. Besides, would Solomon be concerned with searching out petty thieves himself? Benaiah could not forget how he had cheated at the chess game and, because he had a guilty conscience, he was sure that the King intended to accuse him publicly and to disgrace him before the court. He rose.

"Your Majesty," he said. "May I have a few private words with you in the judges' chambers."

"As you wish," King Solomon said courteously.

He and Benaiah left the court and walked into the judges' chambers. Benaiah closed the door. He spun around and grasped Solomon's arm.

"Oh do not punish me in public, O Solomon, I beg of you. I confess it. I confess it all. I moved your knight and I won that chess game dishonorably. Punish me as you will, but I plead with you, do not disgrace me in public."

"Of course I will not humiliate you before the members of the court," Solomon said kindly. "I only wanted you to admit that you did cheat in the game, Benaiah. I only want to know that you know that cheating is wrong."

"Cheating is dreadfully wrong," Benaiah cried. "You know I have never cheated before, Your Majesty. But I was so desperate to win one game from you! So desperate. That's no excuse, oh I know, I know that there is never any excuse for cheating."

"Never." King Solomon shook his head.

"I promise, Your Majesty," Benaiah said. "I shall never cheat again."

"Very well," King Solomon said. "I forgive you."

He turned to open the door leading back into the court. Then, over his shoulder, he said,

"By the way, Benaiah. There *were* real thieves in the palace last night."

"There were!" Benaiah echoed, flushing a bright red as he realized how easily the King led him to betray his own guilt.

"There were," the King said, and smiled. "And I, the King, did apprehend the thieves myself!"

"And I, Benaiah," said Benaiah. "Brought myself to justice. My sense of guilt made me ashamed and when you said you caught a thief, I thought you meant me."

"When we do evil," Solomon said, "the knowledge of our wrong-doing makes us cowards. Walk in the right path and you never need be ashamed."

"I shall never cheat again," Benaiah said. "O wise king, give me of your wisdom. Tell me a Proverb that will keep me from the way of wickedness."

"Here is a Proverb for you," said Solomon the King. "The wicked walk in darkness. They know not at what they stumble."

"I shall not stumble again," said Benaiah. "I shall walk in the light."

The Wagging Tongue

Far off in the land of Persia, the king fell sick. No one knew what disease he had. The Royal Physician was helpless and so were all the other doctors who came to see the King. No one knew how to bring him back to health.

One day a very young physician asked if he could visit the sick monarch. The Royal Physician smiled at this impudence, certain that this young man could not possibly know what wiser physicians had failed to discover. But shrugging his shoulders, he said yes, what could be the harm?

So the young physician went into the King's bedroom and examined him. When he finished, he said to the King,

"I do not know the nature of Your Majesty's illness, but I believe that there is one way to cure it."

"Tell us quickly!" the Royal Physician exclaimed.

The young physician said slowly, "Let the King drink the milk of a lioness."

"The milk of a lioness!" the King gasped from the bed. "A lioness is not a cow. How could anyone ever get near enough to one to milk it!"

142

"There is only one person wise enough to know that," the young physician said. "That person is the wise Solomon, King of Israel."

"Yes, yes," the King of Persia murmured. "King Solomon! If only he could help."

"Let us try," the Royal Physician suggested. "Let us try anything which will save our king."

"Let me go to the land of Israel," the young physician said. "I shall persuade King Solomon to help us."

"Yes, yes," murmured the sick King. "Go, and may the gods speed you there and back."

Four messengers were dispatched with the young physician to go to the land of Israel and ask King Solomon to procure for them the milk of a lioness. They travelled as quickly as possible, and, at length, they reached King Solomon's court. When he heard that a deputation from the Persian court wanted to see him, he sent for them at once.

The four messengers and the physician came into the audience chamber and bowed.

"How fares the King of Persia?" King Solomon asked.

"Poorly, Your Majesty," the physician replied. "The King of Persia is ill and he has sent for your aid."

"Of course," Solomon said quickly. "I am sorry to hear that he is ill, and if there is anything I can do to help him, I shall gladly do it."

"We thank you, Your Majesty," the physician said, bowing low. Then straightening up, he said more boldly. "It has been told the King of Persia, that his sickness will disappear if he will but drink the milk of a lioness."

"The milk of a lioness!" exclaimed Solomon. "I have some lionesses in my Royal Zoo, but no one has ever been able to obtain the milk of a lioness."

The physician bowed low. "That is why we have come to you, O wise Solomon. Our King and the Persian court all agreed that if any one person could know how to get the lioness's milk, it would be Solomon, the wise King of Israel."

King Solomon frowned in thought. Then, waving his hand, he said to his chamberlain,

"Take these men. Feed them. See to their comfort. I must think in peace."

After a little thought, the King summoned Benaiah, and gave him this order:

Every day when it was time for one of the lionesses in the Royal Zoo to be fed her dinner, Benaiah was to go to her cage and he was to put the food into the cage so that she would become accustomed to seeing him. Then perhaps after a week, she would feel friendly enough to let him come close to her and to milk her.

"And if not," Benaiah murmured. "Then she will make a good meal of me."

"Do not fear, Benaiah," King Solomon smiled. "It will go as I have said."

Benaiah went to the cage of the lioness carrying a big piece of red meat. She growled as he neared the cage, stepping forward to protect her young cubs. Benaiah put his hand on the door of the cage. The lioness growled deep in her throat and stalked closer. Benaiah pushed the raw meat through one of the bars and stepped quickly away.

The next day he returned and again as he approached, the lioness growled and moved to protect her cubs. Benaiah pushed the meat through the bars of the cage and again he went away.

He went back the third day. This time the lioness did not growl. She sniffed eagerly at the meat. But Benaiah did not dare open the door of her cage.

He followed this plan of action for seven days. On the morning of the eighth day, when he came, he carried a silver milk pail. This time he took courage and opened the door of the cage. The lioness watched him. He stepped inside. She watched him come. He took two steps toward her, holding out the meat.

One of the servants stood nervously about, whip in hand, ready to protect Benaiah if the lioness turned on him. But in a docile way, she let Benaiah approach her. He put the meat down in front of her and then, without any trouble, she let him milk her.

When he finished, he rubbed his hand gratefully over her neck. She stopped eating, turned her head, purred at him, and returned to her food.

Benaiah backed out of the cage, slowly, step-by-step, careful not to startle her. He held the silver bucket containing the milk tight against him. He stepped out of the cage, closed the door softly, and he and the servants breathed a deep sigh of relief. Then he hurried with the milk to King Solomon who ordered it poured into a golden bottle. The golden bottle was first wrapped in silk, then encased in leather.

144

The Persian physician and the four messengers were brought before the King. Solomon said to the physician,

"I have obtained the milk of a lioness. Here it is. Take it to the King of Persia. And may it speedily restore him to health."

"O good King Solomon," the physician exclaimed. "I thank you. I thank you in the name of the King of Persia. May you, for your kindness, be granted continued health and success."

The physician and the four messengers left Jerusalem hurriedly to return as quickly as possible to their sick King.

On their return journey, one night, while the physician was fast asleep, he had a peculiar dream. He dreamed that the different parts of his body were quarrelling.

"I am the most important part of a man's body," the Feet said. "Because I take him wherever he wants to go."

"Nonsense," said the Hands. "I am more important than you. I feed him his food to keep him alive. I dress his body to keep him warm. I do all the work he has to do."

"Oh, it's too silly to argue about," said the Head. "Where would the Feet be, what could the Hands do, if it weren't that I, the Head, tell the Feet where to go and the Hands what to do. So I say, *I* am supreme."

"And I say I am supreme," shrilled the Tongue. "I can get all of you into trouble. Or I can get all of you out of trouble."

"Quiet, quiet," shouted the Feet and the Head and the Hands.

"I am supreme!" yelled the Tongue.

"Quiet! Quiet!" yelled the Head and the Hands and the Feet.

"I'll prove to you I'm supreme!" shouted the Tongue.

"Quiet! Quiet!" yelled the Hands and the Feet and the Head.

And finally they silenced the too-quick Tongue.

The physician awoke. "What a funny dream," he said, and then he just laughed about it, and forgot it.

On the next day he and the messengers arrived at the Court of the King of Persia. Instantly, without wasting a moment, they went directly to the bedroom of the King. The King lay on the bed, pale and wan and even sicker than when they left.

"Hurry, hurry," he pleaded weakly. "Did you have success?"

"Yes." The physician hurried to the bedside. "Here you are, Your Majesty. I have brought you the milk of a dog."

"What!" shouted everyone in the sickroom.

"The milk of a dog!" croaked the King, as loud as his sick voice could shout. "I sent you for the milk of a lioness and you bring me the milk of a dog! Guards! Arrest this man! He shall be hanged in two days time!"

The physician, pale as the milk he had brought, placed the golden flask with the lioness' milk on an ivory chest, and then was led away by the guard. As soon as he got to the prison cell he fell asleep, and dreamed the same dream of the night before, continuing it as all the members of his body began to shout at the Tongue.

"You ungrateful Tongue! Look what you have done! Why did you have to tell such a lie! Now we are going to hang, all of us together because you uttered such a falsehood."

The Tongue chuckled. "I told you I could get you into trouble, didn't I?"

"Yes, you did," grumbled the Feet. "Now you can just get us out of trouble again."

"Not until you admit that the Tongue is supreme," said the Tongue.

"But I am supreme," yelled the Feet.

"No, I am supreme," yelled the Hands.

"And I say I am supreme," the Head growled.

"Very well," the Tongue said quietly. "Then we all hang together, the supreme Head and the supreme Feet and the supreme Hands."

"Now this is quite foolish," the Hands said. "What good does it do if we all hang? It is much better to stay alive. Yes, I must admit, the Tongue must be supreme. The Tongue got us into this trouble, and it is only this Tongue which can get us out of trouble."

"I don't agree," grumbled the Feet.

"Listen to me," the Hands said. "Suppose we went back to the King, and I showed him how I dress this physician whose hands I am, and I show him how I roll pills, or eat my breakfast. Would that convince the King to forgive the physician and let us live?"

"Ah, I see your point," the Head said. "But if the Tongue went to the King and told him the truth, then he would let us live."

"Quite right," the Hands said.

The Tongue chuckled to himself, letting the others argue for him.

"Yes, I suppose so," grumbled the Feet. "If I went to the King and showed

146

him how I walk, and how I can kick, I don't suppose he'd forgive this foolish physician who lets his tongue tell lies."

"Then you must admit I am supreme," said the Tongue.

"Yes, yes," the others agreed. "But we will only really admit that you are supreme when you get us out of this trouble."

"Very well," the Tongue said.

The Tongue nudged the physician. It whispered to him, "Call the Royal Warden. Have him open the prison gates."

The physician awoke and, remembering his dream, rattled the bars of his dungeon. The Warden, hearing the noise, came running.

"Why such a racket?" he said sternly.

"Please take me to the King," the physician pleaded. "I can still save his life. I must see the King. I must!"

"I don't know," the Warden said doubtfully. "You've been sentenced to hang. I can't just take you out of prison."

"Then go and get permission. Tell the King I remember now how to heal him," the physician urged. "Go. Go. Please hurry."

The jailor turned slowly away, shaking his head, muttering to himself. While he was gone, the physician paced the cell, anxiously hoping he would not be too late to save the King, and also himself. Oh, why had his careless tongue gotten him into such a predicament.

Finally the Warden returned. "No use," he said, shaking his head. "The King doesn't want to see you."

"Oh, I beg of you," pleaded the physician. "If you love the King and want him to live, take me to him."

The Warden, shaking his head in bewilderment all the time, bound the physician's arms in chains and led him to the King.

"O King," the physician pleaded. "Please forgive me for not telling you the truth. There in that flask on that chest is the milk of a lioness which King Solomon gave to me. I beg of you, O King, to drink that milk."

"You now call it the milk of a lioness," said the King. "You think to save your own life."

"No, no, I think only of the King," the physician pleaded. "Put me to death if you wish. But please drink that milk."

"There can be no harm in trying, Your Majesty," the Royal Physician quietly urged.

"Very well," admitted the King, though grudgingly.

The Royal Steward brought the package over to the King, unbound the leather casing, untied the silken wrapping, and from the golden flask into a golden cup, he poured the lioness's milk. The King drank it.

For a few moments, nothing happened. Then, suddenly, he coughed. He raised his head. He sat up. He got out of bed. He stood up straight. He raised his arms above his head. He lifted his head high. He lowered his arms. The color began to flow back into his cheeks.

And suddenly the King was strong and well.

"You did cure me!" he cried out to the young physician. "You did cure me. And I shall let you live. Yes, I shall let you live, and I shall also reward you."

Then the physician's Tongue whispered slyly to his Feet and Hands and Head. "You see, I did get you out of trouble."

And back whispered the Head and the Hands and the Feet, "Now we admit you really and truly are supreme."

The King of Persia ordered a huge ship filled with many costly and precious treasures, and commanded the physician to take them to King Solomon to reward him for saving his life with the milk of a lioness.

When the physician arrived at King Solomon's court and presented him with the gifts from the King of Persia, he told King Solomon the story of his dreams and how his tongue had first betrayed him and then rescued him.

King Solomon smiled, called for his Scribe, and said,

"I have a new Proverb to put into my book. Listen and write this down:
    'Death and life are in the power of the tongue.' "

The Beggar King

When King Solomon was building the Temple, he captured the demon Asmodeus for the main purpose of helping him find the Shamir. Benaiah had brought Asmodeus in chains to the King. This demon had told Solomon how to find the Shamir. And then Asmodeus had been thrown into the dungeon, and there he languished for many years.

One day King Solomon was inspecting his prison with the Royal Warden. Soon they came to the cell occupied by Asmodeus, king of the demons.

"Well, Asmodeus," King Solomon declared. "I confess I almost forgot you were my guest here."

Asmodeus grumbled. "Guest indeed. Sunk in these gloomy dungeons. My eye has forgotten the look of the sun. My face has forgotten the feel of its warmth. I beg you, Your Majesty, not for much — just for a look at the sun."

"That isn't too big a request," King Solomon agreed.

He ordered that Asmodeus, in chains, be brought out to the courtyard.

The Royal Warden opened the door of the cell and led Asmodeus forward, following the King up the steps, out of the dungeon, into the sunlit courtyard. The King dismissed the Warden and he and Asmodeus were alone.

Out in the sunshine, Asmodeus rubbed one chained wrist against the other, looked up at the sun, turned to frown at Solomon and muttered something.

"Speak more clearly," Solomon ordered him.

"A fine keeper of promises you are," muttered Asmodeus loudly. "That's what I said. A fine keeper of promises."

Solomon frowned back at him. "I am the King. How dare you talk to me like that? Besides, I always keep my promises."

"You didn't with me," Asmodeus said. "You promised that if I helped you find the Shamir, with which you could cut the stones from the quarry for the Temple building, you would release me. I helped you find the Shamir. But look at me, still in chains, still your prisoner!"

"True, true," King Solomon said quietly. "But if you are really the king of the demons, as you claim to be, you wouldn't need to be released from a stone prison and iron chains. You would be powerful enough to release yourself."

"Oh, it's fine for you to scorn me thus," Asmodeus said bitterly. "When you stand there in all your glory, and I grovel at your feet, a prisoner. On your finger you wear the magic ring, engraved with the Name. If you would let me wear that ring for one moment, I would show you my power."

"Do you then think that without the ring, I, Solomon, am unable to control you?"

"Yes, I do!" Asmodeus declared.

Solomon frowned. "Indeed. I shall show you the power of Solomon."

He released the chains from Asmodeus' ankles and wrists. Asmodeus rubbed his wrists, groaning loudly, pretending that they were chafed from the iron bands. Then King Solomon removed the magic ring from his own finger and handed it to Asmodeus. Asmodeus put the ring on his little finger.

"Now," said the King. "Let me see how powerful you are."

150

Asmodeus grinned, a most demonish grin, reached over and, without any effort, picked King Solomon up bodily, held him high in the air, while the King struggled to get down. Then Asmodeus shouted, "Farewell, O Solomon," and flung Solomon, far away.

Solomon felt himself flying through the air, rubbing against high rocks which tore at his purple robes, brushing against treetops which ripped his garments. Then, after what seemed like a long, long time, he felt himself dropping, dropping, dropping. And he landed amongst sharp stones and rough branches which scratched him and tore at his skin.

He lay quietly for a long time, recovering his breath and his strength. After a while he sat up, wondering where he was. He struggled to his feet and began to walk, hoping to reach a town quickly. There he would tell the people who he was, find transportation to return him to Jerusalem, and then he would punish that impudent Asmodeus for playing such a trick on him!

Solomon walked a long, long time, bruising his feet, getting wearier and wearier, until finally he came to a town. He asked the first stranger where he was, and when the man told him, Solomon realized he was four hundred miles from home!

He said to this stranger, "I am Solomon, King of Israel."

The man looked at his tattered clothes and his torn shoes, at his dust-covered face and scratched hands, then threw back his head and laughed.

"Ho, ho, how funny, ragged one," he said finally. "You, the King of Israel! Then I am the King of Persia!"

"No, no," Solomon cried, clutching the man's arm. "It is no joke. It is no trick. Listen, please listen. I *am* King Solomon."

The man tore his arm away from the King's grasp, muttered, "Poor demented fool," and strode quickly away.

"What an idiot that man was," Solomon said to himself, "not to recognize me."

Solomon continued on his way. Everywhere he went, he received the same treatment. He tried to tell people he was a King. They looked at his garments and laughed at him. He insisted that he was Solomon, King of Israel, and they thought he was crazy. He asked for help to get back to his own country, and scorn and sneers were his only answers.

And then slowly it dawned on him that there was no way he could prove that he was really and truly King Solomon. His royal garments were tattered.

His noble face was bruised. He had no crown. He had no scepter and he had no money. He soon realized his truly sorry plight when he became hungry and had to beg from door to door, like the most miserable beggar, for a crust of bread, a bowl of soup.

Several days passed. Solomon slept in the open fields. He begged for his food. Then one day, to his delight, he met a rich man who did recognize him.

"Solomon!" the man exclaimed. "King of Israel! What do you, O King, masquerading as a beggar?"

"Oh, my dear friend," Solomon cried joyfully, happy to have found someone who knew him. "This is no masquerade. I have been deposed by a wicked demon and I need help to return to Jerusalem and recover my throne."

"Ah indeed." The man smiled slyly. "So the great King Solomon needs my humble help. There, there, good King," he said smoothly. "Perhaps I can help you. Come with me."

Happily Solomon followed the rich man to a large and magnificent home. He washed the dust and the grime from his face and hands, and then he and his host sat down to a rich banqueting board.

He was so hungry, his mouth actually watered when he saw the roasted brown geese and the fat stewed chickens and the rich white bread. As the platters were passed to him, he helped himself liberally, but, before he could begin to eat, his host began to talk.

"What a fine state of affairs," he said mockingly, "when the once powerful

152

Solomon has to beg from door to door. But eat, my friend eat," he said slyly, pushing a plate of roasted chestnuts before Solomon.

But the man's words reminded him of his truly sorry state, and the food began to taste like ashes in his mouth. He found he could not chew, he could not swallow. All this rich food was being wasted.

"Yes, yes, a great pity," the rich man said, pretending to sigh. "If only your friends could see you now, tattered and torn and shabby. I wonder what the other kings would say if they could see you as I see you. But eat, my friend, eat," he said, pushing a dish of large, juicy peaches in front of Solomon.

The man's scorn and insulting contempt turned the sweet food into bitterness. Angrily, but with dignity, Solomon pushed back his plate, rose from the table, thanked his host politely, and left.

And again he went from door to door, begging a crust of bread.

A few days later Solomon met another man who recognized him. This man, however, was a poor man.

"Your Majesty!" he exclaimed. "What has happened to you? How tired you look, how weary! Please, allow me to extend to you the hospitality of my home. It is a poor home and my food is not rich, but at least there you can rest, there you can . . ."

And still talking softly, sympathetically, the man led Solomon to a very poor but a very clean house. When the man's wife saw who their guest was, she ran to put a clean white cloth on the table, and brought him the best food that they had. It wasn't actually fine food, it was only cheese and bread and some blue grapes, but it *was* the best they had.

They urged the King to come to the table, and to eat, and they refused to say one word to him while he ate. They kept urging him to eat more and more, when he seemed ready to stop. But even more importantly, they showed him such kindness and sympathy, that Solomon's heart was warmed.

When he was ready to leave, the poor man said,

"Do not worry, dear King. God promised that the house of David would rule over Israel. You will yet be restored to your throne."

The poor man's words put fresh courage into the King, and as he left their house, he said to himself,

"Some day when I am back on my throne, I shall write this in my Book of Proverbs: 'It is better to eat a dinner of herbs where there is friendship, than a sumptuous banquet in a home where there is only hate and bitterness.' "

Then the King began his wandering again. For three long years he wandered as a beggar. Finally he came to the city of Ammon in the kingdom east of the Jordan. Dirty and tattered as he was, he nevertheless went to the palace and begged for an audience with the King of Ammon. The guard started to laugh at him, but something noble and commanding in the beggar's presence, made him shrug helplessly, and he led Solomon into the King's presence.

"Whom bring ye here?" the King roared.

"If it please, Your Majesty," Solomon said, bowing low. "I am Solomon, the King of Israel."

"You, Solomon, the King of Israel!"

And the King of Ammon began to laugh, just as everyone had laughed at Solomon these past three, long years.

"Please, please believe me," Solomon begged.

"Oh, this is a very funny joke," the King of Ammon said, wiping away his tears of laughter. "You could never convince me that you are a king of anything," he said finally. "But I'll tell you what. You did amuse me and you look like a good fellow. I'll give you a position in my kitchen as a helper to one of my cooks. And who knows, perhaps some day you will be a king in the kingdom of the dishpans!"

He laughed again, and Solomon knew it was hopeless to try to convince him. But at least a position, even as a cook's helper in the royal household, was certainly better than begging from door to door.

And, indeed, Solomon soon learned to cook and proved to be such a good cook, that before long he became the Head Chef.

Now the king had a beautiful daughter whose name was Naamah. On her birthday, Solomon prepared a delicious cake, and so pleased was she that Naamah wanted to thank the cook herself. So, with her ladies-in-waiting, she went into the kitchen.

The moment Naamah and Solomon looked at each other, they fell deeply in love. Solomon knew theirs was a hopeless love. They could never marry. The King would scorn to give his daughter to a mere cook, nay more, he would order him beheaded for his impudence. But Naamah was firm in her love and fearless and she insisted that they confess their love to the King and ask him for permission to marry.

So, one day they sought an audience with the King. He consented to see them. And they told him of their love and asked his consent to their marriage.

154

For a moment the King stared at them, speechless. Then he roared and raged.

"Marry the Princess! You, a cook! You are a madman, a madman. Guard, arrest this insane creature."

"No, No," Naamah cried. "Father, please, listen to me. He is not a madman. He loves me and I love him . . ."

"Silence," roared the King. "Back to your kitchen, you mad cook."

"But I am not a cook," Solomon insisted. "I am the King of Israel."

"Oh, do you still persist in that crazy idea!" the King of Ammon roared, no longer amused. "No, I say, no! My daughter will not marry a cook, and much less, an insane one!"

He banished Solomon to work in the stables, and shut the princess up in her bedroom until she should come to her senses. But there she did nothing but weep all day. She would not eat. She would not rest. And finally the Queen, fearing that her daughter would fade away before her eyes, pleaded with the King to relent.

When it seemed that the princess really would starve herself to death for the love of Solomon, the King of Ammon summoned both his daughter, the starving and stubborn princess, and Solomon in from the stables.

He said to them, "I still do not want my daughter to marry you. But rather than let her starve to death, I suppose I shall consent."

Solomon and Naamah turned to each other joyously, but the king interrupted.

"But I will not have my court laugh me to scorn over this unsuitable marriage. You may marry, but, immediately after the wedding, you will be banished from my kingdom."

Solomon and Naamah scarcely heard the sentence of exile, so happy were they that they were going to be married.

The wedding was a simple one, simpler even than the poorest maiden could have had. But they didn't care, just so long as they were together.

The King did banish them. He had them taken out to a barren desert. It was a miserable place, and there they might starve. But if they did, at least he would not see them.

Thus the beggar-king, Solomon, monarch of Israel, began once more his life of a wandering beggar. But this time, at his side, to share his trials, there wandered with him the lovely and beautiful Princess Naamah.

The Claw-Hoof

In Jerusalem, at the court of King Solomon, his trusty lieutenant, Benaiah, sat one day brooding over the strange behavior of the King. Why was it that Solomon never consulted with him any more? He and the King used to play chess every evening, but it had been many months since they had sat over the chess board. Months, Benaiah thought. No! It was years. Besides, the King ignored everyone in the court and nowadays, whenever he heard law suits, he seemed to take a fiendish delight in deciding them in favor of the guilty one. Everyone in the court was perplexed, but no one as much as Benaiah.

What neither he nor anyone else in the kingdom knew was that the king who ruled in Jerusalem was not Solomon but Asmodeus, who had disguised himself, with the help of the magic ring, to look like Solomon.

Every day Asmodeus would put the magic ring on his little finger. It never went on beyond the first knuckle because it was too small for his thick finger. Then he would seat himself on Solomon's Magic Tapestry and go sailing around the country.

156

One day he stepped onto the carpet, clapped his hands, said,
"Rise! To Arabia!"

He had decided to ride over the country to see if he could spy out King Solomon. What fun it would be, he chuckled to himself, to see how that stupid king was getting along now that he had only his own wits to guide him. He, Asmodeus, had the magic ring, and Solomon had nothing but his own supposed wisdom. Oho, hee hee, Asmodeus chuckled, he must have had a hard time of it. How I would like to catch a glimpse of him.

Asmodeus sat very close to the edge of the carpet, leaning over, scanning the ground below. Then, as the Magic Tapestry turned homeward, it turned to the sea and began to cross it. The carpet gave a little lurch and Asmodeus reached out to clutch the edge of it to keep from falling off. And the sharp edge of the carpet pulled the ring off his finger!

Down it fell, down, down to the sea. Asmodeus did not notice. Scrambling back to the center of the tapestry, he was so relieved to find himself safe, he didn't discover that the ring was gone.

The ring floated down to the water, struck the waves and began to sink. Along came a big fish and reached for it, thinking it was food. The fish swallowed the ring, and went on swimming along.

Now off in the desert where the King of Ammon had banished them, Solomon and his new wife Naamah were struggling to keep alive. They kept journeying onward, hoping to reach a village. Finally they did, at the shore of the sea. They did not have to beg for their food yet, because the Princess was wearing a beautiful topaz necklace. They sold it, and for several weeks they were able to eat comfortably from the sale of the necklace.

Finally the day came when they had eaten up all the food and had no more money. But the Princess still owned a ring set with a black pearl. For this they were able to get quite a large sum of money. That day, after they sold the ring, they hid most of the money in their little hut in which they lived, and went out to the market to buy some food.

The Princess wanted to buy a goose, but Solomon insisted they buy a fish instead. So at the fish market they selected a nice, large, fat-looking fish and took it home to cook. While the Princess was cleaning the fish and preparing it for cooking, she exclaimed in surprise.

Solomon came to see what had startled her, and there, in the fish, was his magic ring! With a cry of joy, he pounced on it, cleaned it off, set it on his finger and said,

"This is my ring, my magic ring. Beware, Asmodeus, the King comes to reclaim his kingdom!"

He and Naamah laughed for joy, and Solomon said,

"Come, my dear Naamah. To Jerusalem we shall go, to the land of Israel where I shall be King and you shall be Queen!"

They started out immediately, using some of their money for horses to ride on, and they travelled as fast as they could. When they reached Jerusalem, they went directly to the palace.

To the guard at the gate, Solomon commanded,

"Open the gate, for the King of Israel."

The guard looked at the ragged traveller, and smiled. "Get you gone, old man, before they throw you into the royal dungeon for pretending to be the king."

"I am the King! Call Benaiah. He will recognize me."

The guard was a good-natured fellow and didn't like to argue with this strange man, so he sent a messenger to call Benaiah to come to the palace gates.

When Benaiah came, Solomon ran forward and grasped his arm.

"Benaiah! Benaiah! Say you recognize me!"

Benaiah stared at the beggarly-looking man, and said slowly, "Who do you say you are?"

"I am the King. I am Solomon, the son of David."

"Indeed, you look like the King," Benaiah said slowly. "But the King sits on his throne in the audience chamber."

"No, no, that is Asmodeus, disguised as me," Solomon said impatiently.

Benaiah struggled, not knowing whether to believe this man who *did* look like Solomon, not knowing whether he was an impostor, to be thrown into the dungeon.

"And who are you," he asked, turning to Naamah.

"I am the Princess of Ammon. I am the wife of this man."

"And who do you say he is?" Benaiah asked.

"He was the chief cook in my father's palace," Naamah said slowly. "So I know him as my father's cook. But as my husband, I know he must be who he says he is. I believe that he *is* Solomon, King of Israel."

"Do you recognize this ring?" Solomon asked Benaiah.

158

Then Benaiah was puzzled. How could this impostor have possession of the King's ring?

"I do not know," he said honestly. "I cannot decide this myself. I shall have to ask the Sanhedrin to help me decide."

"Ask them," Solomon said impatiently. "All seventy men of the court will recognize me."

Benaiah arranged to hide Solomon and Naamah in a secret room of the palace. Then he went to Asmodeus who was disguised as Solomon. Asmodeus was sitting on the throne, looking gloomily out of the window, worrying about the magic ring. He could not remember where he had put it last, or if he had lost it. He had looked everywhere imaginable and could not find it. Without the ring he could not complete his disguise. He was in danger of some one's recognizing the one tell-tale thing that would betray his identity. He had better find that ring.

And so he was deep in gloomy thought when Benaiah came into the audience chamber. The moment Asmodeus saw him, he pulled his feet in quickly, hiding them under his robe, under the throne.

Benaiah bowed, and said,

"Your Majesty, a most important matter has come up for decision. I beg leave to assemble the Sanhedrin here within the hour. I ask that your Majesty sit as judge with the Sanhedrin."

"Very well, very well," Asmodeus said impatiently, eager to get Benaiah out of his sight so he could start thinking again and perhaps recall where he had left the ring.

Benaiah left, and Asmodeus worried. Benaiah worked fast. He assembled the whole of King Solomon's court and the Sanhedrin in less than an hour. Asmodeus was surprised to see that Benaiah had assembled the courtiers as well, but he said nothing, absorbed as he was in his worry over the ring.

When everyone was in place and quiet reigned, Benaiah gave a signal, and the guard at the door ushered in Solomon and Naamah, still dressed in their ragged clothes. Solomon kept the hand wearing the ring out of sight behind his back. The moment Asmodeus saw him enter, Asmodeus carefully kept his feet out of sight, under his robes.

"Whom bring ye here!" he shouted.

Solomon and Benaiah faced the court, and Benaiah said slowly,

"I bring a man who claims to be King Solomon!"

A great hubbub arose, everyone talking at once, but Asmodeus shouted them all down.

"Away with this impostor!" he yelled. "To prison with him. And to the gallows!"

"Yes, truly," a nobleman called out. "I cannot imagine why you brought him here, Benaiah. Why would you have dealings with an impostor?"

Benaiah raised his hand, and when all fell silent, he said,

"I brought him here because . . ."

He nodded to Solomon who held up the hand wearing the ring.

"Because he wears the King's magic ring."

Again there was excitement in the court, a harsh murmuring of voices, and again Asmodeus shouted them down.

"The ring was stolen from me! That man is a thief."

Then Solomon stepped forward and when everyone saw that he was about to speak, they fell silent again.

He bowed slightly. "It is true that I could have stolen this ring. But I did not. It rightfully belongs to me. But I have another proof that I am King, Solomon, son of David, and that he," pointing to Asmodeus, "is the king only of the demons. He is Asmodeus, and I am Solomon."

"What is your proof?" Asmodeus said, swaggering a little, though his cheeks turned pale.

Solomon smiled. "Many of the men in this court have gone swimming with me in the river. They have seen my feet. They know my feet look just like the feet of all men. But that monster . . ."

H turned and stared at Asmodeus.

"Asmodeus," he commanded. "Let us see your feet."

"Nonsense!" Asmodeus sputtered. "Am I king or a slave to be ordered about by a beggar? Away with him! To prison with him! Away, away!" he shrieked.

"Let us see *your* feet," one nobleman called out to Solomon.

"Certainly."

Solomon bent over, loosened the sandals off his feet. Everyone present looked and saw feet, just like any other feet.

Then Benaiah ran up the steps of the throne and pulled Asmodeus's feet out from under his robes before he could protest.

160

And then they saw . . . instead of feet . . . they saw a claw-hoof, the sign of the demon!

"It *is* Asmodeus!" someone cried.

Asmodeus, with a great shriek, threw off Benaiah's hand, and in a twinkling, before the court realized what was happening, he disappeared from sight.

But no one cared. As long as he was gone, they didn't worry about him. They all crowded around Solomon, welcoming him home.

Benaiah led him and Naamah to the throne. And Solomon, the son of David, was King once more.

The Golden Trees

Many kings of the east helped King Solomon build his Temple. The King of Egypt sent skilled workmen. Hiram, the King of Tyre, cut the cedars in the forests of Lebanon and floated them in rafts. Asmodeus, the King of the Demons, told Solomon how to find the Shamir which he needed to cut the heavy stones. From the Phoenicians came skilled workmen, and Solomon used whatever help he could find, because he wanted to make the Temple as magnificent as was possible.

It took seven years to build and during that time not one single workman, not one person connected with the building, fell sick. When it was completed, King Solomon invited all the neighboring kings and nobles to come and see it. All came and all were loud in their praise.

The King of Egypt admired the ten candlesticks and the ten tables almost as much as the architecture. But Hiram, King of Tyre, was warmest in his praise of the gardens. He walked slowly, examining each exotic plant, admiring, praising, and finally he said,

"But my good friend, Solomon. All these exotic plants! How can you possibly expect to grow these rare plants out of their native soil?"

"That is no problem." King Solomon smiled. "One of my eagles flies to India every other day. And from India he brings the water to keep these plants alive."

"Wonderful, wonderful," Hiram murmured in amazement. "And these balsam trees. Where did you secure these balsams?"

King Solomon turned to the Queen of Sheba who was walking on his right side. She had come that great distance to be present at the dedication. Now he bowed to her.

"The balsam trees are the gracious gift of the fair Queen of Sheba."

"Gracious, indeed," Hiram agreed, and he too bowed to the Queen.

She curtsied to the two kings.

The procession continued and Solomon said, "But see here, Hiram." Solomon took him by the arm. "Let me show you some other trees."

"They can't be more unusual than these plants and the balsams," Hiram protested, walking along with Solomon.

162

Solomon smiled and said nothing. He led him and the Queen of Sheba to a grove of trees and his guests exclaimed aloud. Hiram almost stuttered as he said,

"Gold trees! Trees of gold! I don't believe my eyes. Now, Solomon, you're just playing a trick. Confess now. Those trees aren't real gold. You just gilded some natural trees."

"No," Solomon said. "These trees are made of gold, all the way through."

They were magnificent, gleaming in the sunlight, and Hiram, who loved gold more than anything else, was filled with envy. The trunks of the trees were gold through and through. The leaves were golden, and firm and steady and on the golden stems, golden fruit blossomed, sending off a rare perfume.

"Oh, I should like to have one of these trees," Hiram said wistfully. "Good friend Solomon, give me one of your gold trees."

"No, I'm sorry, Hiram," Solomon said. "That I cannot do. These trees are for the glory of the Temple. They must stand here as long as the Temple stands."

"Then," said Hiram, "the trees will remain here forever, since the Temple will stand forever, for the Temple is indestructible."

"I pray to God it is as you say," Solomon said.

Hiram sighed. "But how I should like to have one."

"It grieves me not to grant your wish, friend Hiram," said Solomon. "Let me instead give you as a gift a column of gold."

"A column of gold!" Hiram's eyes gleamed. "Ah splendid. That's splendid of you, Solomon. And I shall make a statue of it for my god Baal."

Solomon frowned. "I'd rather you put it to the worship of the One God, than to an idol. But then, if I give you a gift, I have no right to tell you how to use it."

Hiram laughed. "Fear not, friend Solomon. I will not offend you and your worship of the One God. I shall use the column of gold for a statue of my lovely daughter instead."

Solomon smiled. "Good. That is better. And my golden trees will remain unique in God's Temple."

After the festivities ended, Solomon, knowing how envious many people would be of these rare and beautiful trees, never took any chances. He detailed a special guard to surround the golden trees to safeguard them from thieves. And the golden trees bloomed and waxed brilliant throughout all of Solomon's lifetime.

Even after he died, the trees remained sturdy and golden, shedding their splendor around the Temple. For four hundred and ten years they shed their radiance. Even through the reign of the wicked Queen Athaliah, who made the people worship the trees instead of God, the golden trees prospered and blossomed. Even when the cruel King Menasseh made the people bow down to the gods of Assyria, even then the golden trees stayed alive. Throughout Hezekiah's reign, and Josiah's, whoever entered the courtyard of the Temple, was struck anew with the beauty of Solomon's golden trees.

Then came the Babylonian conqueror, Nebuchadnezzar. He laid siege to Jerusalem, captured the city, and drove the Israelites in chains into Babylonian captivity. He ordered his soldiers to destroy the Temple.

He found the secret, underground passage which Solomon had built and in which Hezekiah had hidden most of the Temple vessels, the ten candlesticks, the ten tables and the sacred Ark. He didn't find all the subterranean passages, but only one. There were two others he knew nothing of. Years later Alexander the Great found the second one. But Nebuchadnezzar found only one passage and plundered it of its treasures. And then his soldiers destroyed the Temple.

Nebuchadnezzar, looking all about him, saw that his work of destruction was complete. The city was demolished. The people were driven into slavery. The Temple was destroyed.

"My work is finished," he said. "But for one more thing. Now I shall possess Solomon's Golden Trees. I shall uproot them, take them to Babylon and plant them in the courtyard of the temple of Marduk, my god."

He himself led a detachment of soldiers out to the courtyard to uproot the Golden Trees.

There in the garden remained one guard who, miraculously, had not been killed in all the fierce fighting. Through all of it he had remained at his post, guarding the Golden Trees. He stood stiff as a rod, white-faced, watching Nebuchadnezzar approach.

Nebuchadnezzar's smile of triumph changed to a frown of anger. He looked all about the garden, then at the poor, white-faced guard, and then he shouted,

"The trees! The golden trees! Where are they?"

The guard pointed a trembling finger at mounds of green ashes.

"There, Your Majesty," he quavered. "There are the golden trees."

"Those green ashes!" shouted Nebuchadnezzar. "Don't lie to me. Who stole the trees?"

"Your Majesty, hear me," the guard pleaded. "Before your soldiers went into the Temple, the trees waxed golden as always, and the fruit of them smelled sweeter than honey. I was guarding the trees, Your Majesty, as I have always guarded them. Then suddenly from inside the Temple, I heard crashing sounds."

"Aye," grumbled Nebuchadnezzar. "I ordered my soldiers to destroy the Temple."

The guard said stiffly, "As soon as the crashing sounds were heard, the golden trees began to wither. Please, Your Majesty, I saw it with my own eyes. The leaves trembled and turned brown and the fruit fell and decayed, and all of the trees, the branches, the fruits, the trunks all shriveled and died and before my very eyes, they turned into green dust!"

Nebuchadnezzar kicked at a pile of green ashes and grumbled. "I wanted those golden trees."

The guard said timidly, "It has always been said, Your Majesty, that Solomon's golden trees would last as long as the Temple stood. The Temple is ruined . . ."

He was afraid to say more.

"And the trees are withered," Nebuchadnezzar said gloomily.

He turned and stared at the ruined Temple, turned again and looked at the green ashes, and walked away to begin his journey back to Babylon.

The Temple had stood for four hundred and ten years. For four centuries the golden trees planted by Solomon had thrived and bloomed in rare beauty. Now the Temple was destroyed. The golden trees were withered. The green ashes mingled with the dust of the earth and waited for the day when the Temple would be built again.

The Travelling Throne

All the kings of the world envied Solomon, the King of Israel. They were jealous of his power. They longed for his wisdom and were greedy for his wealth. But above all else, they envied him his wonderful throne.

Hiram, king of Tyre, would have liked to possess it because of the fine gold with which it was made and the precious jewels it contained. He offered Solomon one thousand slaves and one thousand more.

But Solomon would not sell his throne, not for three thousand more.

The Pharaoh of Egypt, who worshipped animals, would have liked to own the throne because of the golden animals on the steps leading to the seat of the throne. He offered Solomon one hundred bushels of costly gems, and one hundred more.

But Solomon would not sell his throne, not for three hundred more.

The King of Persia would have liked to possess the throne because of the wonderful machinery which made the animals coo and howl and shriek and which made it possible for the golden lions to lead Solomon up the steps to the top of the throne. The King of Persia offered Solomon five hundred miles of river-land and five hundred more.

166

But Solomon would not sell the throne, even for fifteen hundred more.

Every king tried to buy it. They offered to give him gifts far more costly in exchange for the throne, but he would not part with it.

The years passed. Solomon aged, and died. And from that time on, the throne went on many an adventurous journey . . .

At Solomon's death, his son Rehoboam became King of Israel. Now when Solomon had first become king, he had married the Egyptian Princess. Her father, Shishak, had always wanted Solomon's throne. The moment Solomon died, Shishak thought of a scheme to get it away from Rehoboam.

"Your father," he said to Rehoboam, "owed me one thousand talents of silver."

"One thousand talents of silver!" exclaimed Rehoboam. "That is a vast sum, sir."

"It is indeed," Shishak agreed. "But he always needed money, you know, for the many buildings he built."

"But I cannot repay such a vast amount of money," Rehoboam said. "It would completely ruin me."

"Well, I would not want to ruin you," Shishak said. He pretended to think deeply. Then he said, "I know how we can settle this debt. It doesn't mean much to me you know, it will really be a sacrifice on my part . . ." He pretended to hesitate, then sighed, and said, "Yes, I am willing to sacrifice the money. If you will give me Solomon's throne, I will cancel the debt."

167

"Oh, that is generous of you," Rehoboam said. "I thank you very much."

Shishak smiled to himself because Solomon had never owed him any money, but Rehoboam had been easy to fool, and now the throne was his! He carted it off to Egypt and set it up in his throne-room. But he did not use it as a throne. The Egyptians worshipped all animals as gods and Shishak used Solomon's throne as an altar. The golden lions and the golden eagles, the peacock and the falcon and the wolf which were on Solomon's throne, those Shishak now worshiped as gods.

Years later the Assyrian king, Sennacherib, declared war on Egypt. He sent a powerful army against the Egyptians. When his generals reported that victory was his, Sennacherib clapped his hands and said,

"One thing I want more than any other object. Bring me Solomon's throne."

His general detailed a group of forty of his soldiers to carry it away from Egypt on their shoulders, and death to any man who so much as scratched it!

As Sennacherib watched his soldiers carry the throne before him, he strutted, proud as a peacock.

"Now I am the most wonderful king in the world," he boasted. "I have power and might and glory. I have a vast army and have conquered many kings. And now I, Sennacherib, I possess the throne of Solomon."

But Sennacherib did not go directly home. On the way back from Egypt, he decided to war against Hezekiah, King of Israel. He could easily have defeated Hezekiah, but he grew careless because of his pride in his strength. Instead of attacking Jerusalem immediately, he let his army dally at Nob, feasting and celebrating in advance. Hezekiah took advantage of Sennacherib's carelessness and, instead of waiting to be attacked, he took the offensive, utterly routing Sennacherib's forces.

The Assyrian king, dazed by this sudden defeat, deserted his army in the midst of battle. He ran away, leaving behind him the wonderful throne of Solomon.

When Hezekiah cleaned out Sennacherib's camp, he found Solomon's throne, unscratched, untouched and in perfect condition. Thus Solomon's throne returned to Solomon's land. And there it stayed for many years.

When Josiah reigned in Jerusalem, the Pharaoh Necho waged war against

Israel. And again the Egyptians were victorious. Necho summoned Josiah to appear before him in chains. Then he said,

"As the conqueror, I shall take Solomon's throne as my prize."

So once more the throne travelled from Jerusalem to Egypt. Pharaoh Necho ordered it put into his throne-room.

"I shall not worship the golden animals on the throne," he said to his court. "Nor shall I use it as an altar. But I shall use it as Solomon used it, as a throne. As the golden animals escorted Solomon to the seat of the throne, so shall they escort me, the Pharaoh of Egypt."

His eyes gleamed with greed to see the gold and precious jewels, and the wonderful golden animals. He looked around at his court to see that everyone watched him mount the throne of Solomon in splendor. Then he turned and began to walk up the steps towards the throne. The moment he did, one of the golden lions reached out to lead him to the throne as it had done with Solomon. The Pharaoh was expecting it but still it frightened him. He yelled in surprise and lurched against the lion which hit him sharply on the leg. It was a bad blow and injured the Pharaoh severely. He fell to the ground and his courtiers ran forward to help him to his bed. He lay helpless on his bed for many months and when he did arise and walk again, it was always with a bad limp. The first time he appeared in public, he heard the people whisper,

"There goes Necho, the hobbler. There goes Necho, the Lame Pharaoh."

"Never call me Necho," he shouted in fury. "I am not lame. I do not hobble," said he, hobbling away.

Never again did he try to sit on Solomon's throne.

Years passed. Nebuchadnezzar mounted the throne in Babylon. He became a powerful monarch and wanted to rule the world. So he decided to wage war against Egypt.

His mighty armies were victorious, and now Nebuchadnezzar came into possession of Solomon's wonderful throne. He had it carefully brought to Babylon. And he, like Necho of Egypt, decided he would use it as his own throne.

But before he had a chance to use it, Nebuchadnezzar marched against Jerusalem. He destroyed the Temple. He laid the city in ruins. He led the people captive to Babylon.

Back home again in his palace, he looked again at Solomon's throne and determined to make it his chief throne. That would be the throne on which he would sit on the most important state occasions.

But Nebuchadnezzar, unlike Necho, knew nothing about the wonderful machinery inside of it. The first time he tried to walk up the six steps to the throne, the lion on the first step dealt him such a severe blow on his left foot, that it lamed him for life, and never again did he dare try to use the throne.

When Darius was King of the Medes and the Persians, the throne of Solomon found its way to Elam. Darius had had great respect for Solomon, the great King of Israel, and when the wondrous throne became his, he had it set up in his throne-room. And to his court he said,

"No one is ever to sit on this throne. Not even I shall mount these steps. We shall carefully preserve the wonderful throne of the mighty Solomon."

Now in Darius' court there was a young Hebrew by the name of Zerubbabel. He found such favor with the king that one day Darius said to him,

"Zerubbabel, you have been faithful to me for many years. And I wish to reward you. Is there any way in which I can show you my gratitude?"

Zerubbabel bowed and then smiled. "There is, Your Majesty, but it is so big a thing to ask, that I hesitate to speak."

"Speak," said Darius. "If it is possible, I shall grant your wish."

Zerubbabel spoke slowly, "Then, Your Majesty, grant me this boon. Let the people of Israel return to Jerusalem and rebuild the Temple of Solomon which Nebuchadnezzar destroyed."

"I will gladly permit that," Darius said. "And I shall give you the treasures of the Temple which Nebuchadnezzar had stolen and which are in my possession. I shall send skilled artisans and workmen to help you in the task of rebuilding the Temple."

"Thank you, Your Majesty, thank you," Zerubbabel said. "And now, even though you have granted me so magnificent a boon —" he paused and smiled. "I have one more favor to ask."

Darius laughed and leaned forward. "Still another favor? Very well, Zerubbabel, I am putty in your hands today. Ask and it is yours."

Zerubbabel stood tall and straight and smiled proudly. "Your Majesty, the throne of Solomon which you possess . . ."

Everyone in the court room turned to look at the magnificent throne, and Darius said,

170

"The throne which no one may occupy."

"That throne," said Zerubbabel, "which was built by the King of Israel. Now that you have been so generous to our people, Your Majesty, we would have pleasure to see you mount that throne."

Darius said nothing, looked at Zerubbabel for a moment, then he looked at the throne. He rose, descended from his throne, walked over to Solomon's throne and put his foot on the first step. The golden Lion came forward and just as respectfully as it had ever escorted Solomon, it led Darius to the seat of the throne.

The court broke into a cheer. And thereafter, Darius occupied the throne of Solomon.

171

No man after Darius ever mounted the throne which had been fashioned for the King of Israel in the city of Jerusalem. It came next to Ahasuerus. But this Persian king had heard how Necho of Egypt had been lamed by the golden lions and how Nebuchadnezzar of Babylon had been crippled by them. So he was afraid to use it as a throne. Instead, he put his architects and his builders to work, to make him one as wonderful, as marvelous. Long years they labored over this work, but time and again they failed. Never again was any craftsman able to make even a fair copy of Solomon's wonderful throne.

From the land of Persia, the throne came into the possession of Alexander the Macedonian. But Alexander the Great was too busy conquering the world to have time to use the throne. It satisfied his vanity merely to know that he owned it.

The throne was next heard of during the time of the Maccabees. Antiochus Epiphanes, the Syrian-Greek who later was defeated by Judah Maccabeas and his brothers, came into possession of Solomon's throne. He wanted to send it to Greece, and directed it to be put aboard a ship. But the workmen were careless in handling it and one of the legs of the throne was loosened from its golden chain. When it was safely in Greece, Antiochus ordered artist after artist to repair the throne, but never was any artist or any goldsmith able to mend the golden chain and the leg of the throne.

Finally, after centuries, the wandering throne came to its last resting-place. Greece was vanquished by Rome, and the throne was carried to Italy, and there in Rome it remained until the Vandals captured and sacked that great city. The Vandals then came into possession of the throne. But where the Vandals carried it, no one knows. Somewhere the throne of Solomon is hidden, awaiting the glorious future.

The Secret Passages

When King Solomon was building the Temple in Jerusalem, he had a secret conference one day with his Master Builder, Hiram.

"Hiram," said the King. "I want you to build two secret passages in the Temple. And I stress the word *secret*. I want no one to know of them. Can you do this for me?"

"Yes, Your Majesty," Hiram said. "I shall construct them myself and no one will ever know about them."

"Thank you, Hiram," the King said. "I knew I could count on you."

"Tell me, Your Majesty," said Hiram, "what you want them for and I shall know how big to build them."

"The first passage," said Solomon, "should be big enough so that in time of danger we may hide in it all the treasures of the Temple."

"You mean the sacred Ark?" asked Hiram.

"Yes," said Solomon. "And the ten tables and the ten candlesticks, all the Temple treasures."

Hiram made a few notes on a parchment scroll, and then he said,

"And what is the second underground passage to be used for, Your Majesty?"

"For the books of wisdom," Solomon said. "My books and the wisdom of men who went before me. Listen to me, Hiram. When I was a lad, I had a most unusual dream. In this dream God offered me one great wish, and my wish was for the gift of Wisdom. Part of the wisdom that was given to me taught me to learn from everything and from everybody, and to write it all down for future ages."

"Ah yes." Hiram nodded. "Real wisdom is not the discovery of one man."

"No," said Solomon. "It is gathered from many people in many ages. Therefore when I began to write my books, I did not begin with my own times. Listen to what I have learned from other people."

Then Solomon the King told Hiram the Builder how Abraham gave to the world the great lesson of hospitality. In that lesson of hospitality, he taught that all men are brothers. And Abraham taught the world, too, that there is only One God.

Here Hiram interrupted. "But, Your Majesty, that is not a difficult lesson. We all know that there is only One God."

"Ah," said King Solomon. "Now we know it, but that was a very difficult idea for men to grasp in the days when Abraham lived. In those far-off days, men worshiped many gods. They had a god of war and a god of the ocean. To one god they prayed for riches and to another for long life. But Abraham brought his teaching of One God and united all of life under One Great Influence. That Divine promise: 'All the peoples of the earth shall find their blessings in thee,' was brought from Abraham by his son Isaac to his son Jacob to the twelve tribes of Israel."

Then Hiram heard from Solomon how Moses, the first of the great teachers and prophets, taught the world to value liberty. When Moses led his enslaved people out of the land of the Pharaohs, he showed them how to search always for freedom. At Mount Sinai Moses gave the people Ten Great Words, the Ten Commandments, to teach them how to live as children of God under God's laws. Murder was outlawed and robbery was forbidden. All the cruelties of the pagan peoples were to be wiped away by the command to love thy neighbor as thyself.

"Your Majesty," Hiram said to Solomon. "And what of the writings of your own father, King David? He wrote the Psalms, the most beautiful prayer-poetry ever written."

King Solomon nodded. "In this secret passage, I shall put a copy of my father's Psalms, and the books I have written."

"Your great love poem, *The Song of Songs?*" asked Hiram.

"Yes," said Solomon. "And the wisdom book, *The Book of Proverbs* and *Kohelet*. I have written on mathematics, Hiram, and astronomy and medicine and many things about precious stones which I have learned."

"All these wonderful writings must be preserved for the future," said Hiram. "I shall construct two good secret passages, King Solomon."

174

And he did. No one knew anything about them, and all through Solomon's reign, the treasures of the Temple and the wisdom Solomon had gathered and had written down were safe in their subterranean hideaways.

After Solomon died, one misfortune after another descended upon the people of Israel. Terrible wars reduced their numbers. Constant pillage levelled their towns.

Then came Nebuchadnezzar who destroyed the Temple. He found one of the two of King Solomon's secret subterranean passages, the one containing all of the sacred Temple vessels. Nebuchadnezzar took these treasures and carted them off to Babylon.

Then out of Macedonia rose the conqueror, Alexander the Great, who swept over the eastern world, conquering great kings and great kingdoms. During one of his campaigns he came to Jerusalem. One of the first things he did was to visit the ruined Temple. In the ruins he discovered the second subterranean passage and in that secret hiding-place, he found all the writings of King Solomon.

Alexander's teacher, Aristotle, lived in Greece. He was one of the greatest thinkers the world has ever known. The Greeks, next to the Judeans, were the greatest lovers of learning.

It was to this land of learning and art, then, and to this great philosopher, Aristotle, that Alexander the Great sent the writings of King Solomon which he had discovered in Jerusalem.

Aristotle read them and taught them and spread the knowledge of the wise King of Israel over the world. What the Greeks taught, the rest of the world hungered to know.

Thus did the wisdom of Solomon, which prompted him to ask Hiram the Builder to erect secret passages in which to hide the books of wisdom, remain concealed until Alexander the Great and Aristotle revealed them to the world. All of the wisdom of Solomon, based on the wisdom of the Prophets and leaders of Israel, spread the knowledge of the One God and His law of mercy over the world.

Thus ends the story of King Solomon who had asked God for the gift of wisdom. His wisdom led him to learn from Abraham and Moses and Samuel and David, his father. His wisdom was written down as an inheritance to all the world and the world has always benefitted, because once Solomon had a dream and in that dream he asked for the gift of wisdom.